ST PATRICK

The Life and World of Ireland's Saint

J. B. Bury

Foreword by
Thomas Charles-Edwards

TAURIS PARKE
PAPERBACKS

Published in 2010 by I.B.Tauris & Co Ltd
6 Salem Road, London W2 4BU
175 Fifth Avenue, New York NY 10010
www.ibtauris.com

Distributed in the United States and Canada Exclusively by Palgrave Macmillan
175 Fifth Avenue, New York NY 10010

ISBN: 978 1 84885 187 0

A full CIP record for this book is available from the British Library
A full CIP record is available from the Library of Congress

Library of Congress Catalog Card Number: available

Printed and bound in India by Thomson Press India Ltd

CONTENTS

CHAPTER IX

CHAPTER X

MAPS

FOREWORD

JOHN Bagnell Bury, born on 16 October 1861, was the son of a Church of Ireland clergyman, Edward John Bury. The father served his ministry in the diocese of Clogher, first as curate of Monaghan, where he found a wife from the same town, Anna Rogers, and then as rector of Clontibret, south-west of Monaghan. Fifteen miles east–north-east of Monaghan and north-east of Clontibret is Armagh, the see which, ever since the seventh century at least, has traced its origins to St Patrick. Edward Bury was a classical scholar and introduced his son to the classical languages from an age at which most children are barely beginning to read. When he went to Trinity College, Dublin, in 1878, he distinguished himself primarily as a classicist, but also in philosophy. In 1885 he became a Fellow of Trinity. His first publications were editions of the Greek poet Pindar, but he soon began publishing important work on Greek and Roman (including Byzantine) history. In 1893 Bury was appointed Professor of Modern History at Trinity and, in 1898, Regius Professor of Greek; he held both posts concurrently until, in 1902, he was appointed Regius Professor of Modern History at Cambridge.

It was at this stage of his career, when he was leaving Ireland, that he began publishing a series of articles on

St Patrick. His edition of Gibbon's *Decline and Fall* had come out between 1896 and 1900 and his *History of Greece to the Death of Alexander the Great* had been published in 1900. These years, when he was in his late thirties, were a period of exceptional productivity; and, by the time he began working on his *Life of St Patrick*, he was already one of the leading historians of his generation in Europe. He was a vigorous advocate of the view that history was a science – something that he explains and defends against criticism in his preface to the *Life of St Patrick* – and a confessed non-Christian ever since his early twenties. One can gain a sense of his independence of thought and his certainty that the claims of historical truth came before any solicitude for his university or family background in what he wrote in his preface to the *Life of St Patrick* written by an earlier luminary of Trinity College, Dublin, J. H. Todd. He criticises Todd for two things: his lack of a systematic analysis of the sources and for 'an unmistakable ecclesiastical bias'. Bury's claim was that he himself, by contrast, had based it on 'a methodical examination of the sources' and that he was wholly free of any sectarian bias. He then goes on to write, 'I will not anticipate my conclusions here, but I may say that they tend to show that the Roman Catholic conception of St Patrick's work is, generally, nearer to historical truth that the views of some anti-Papal divines.' It was hardly surprising that Bury's version of Patrick came to be cherished by Catholic scholars.

The cover of the first edition gives the title as *Life of St Patrick*, but the title page adds a second phrase *and His Place in History*. Chapter 1 is entitled 'On the Diffusion of Christianity beyond the Roman Empire', while the final

chapter is 'Patrick's Place in History'. These give a clue as
to Bury's reasons for setting about studying St Patrick: he
came to it as an ancient historian with a particular interest
in the Late Empire and its Byzantine or East-Roman heir.
Patrick's role in spreading Christianity beyond the bounds of
the Empire is compared with those of Wulfilas, the apostle
of the Goths north of the lower Danube, Nino, the 'enlightener and apostle of Georgia', and Frumentius, the first
bishop of Axum in Ethiopia. Bury approached the career of
St Patrick as an episode in the history of the world. This is
an abiding strength of the book: we now know much more
about the early history of Ireland but later students of Patrick have hardly had Bury's breadth of outlook. One of his
most enduring later works has been his last major book, a
two-volume *History of the Later Roman Empire from the Death
of Theodosius I to the Death of Justinian*. This was a detailed
account of only part of the period covered by an earlier work,
published in 1888, *A History of the Later Roman Empire from
Arcadius to Irene (A.D. 395 to A.D. 800)*. Patrick's career fell
within the period covered by these two works and the *Life*
is an offshoot of Bury's Late-Roman interests. A historian
of the Roman Empire must necessarily range from Persia
to Britain; no narrow specialization on the history of one
nation is possible. Patrick was, after all, the only one of these
apostles of Christianity beyond the Empire to leave us texts
written by himself bearing directly on aspects of his mission.
His significance was much wider than the history of Ireland.

Bury, as we have seen, aspired to write 'scientific history'.
'The business of a historian', he declares in the preface to the
Life, 'is to ascertain facts'. Yet verifiable facts are hard to come

by when studying the career of St Patrick. His own writings are better guides to the man rather than his deeds. Bury, however, was first and foremost concerned with deeds; he was no scrutiniser of the human soul, as is clear from the single paragraph that he devoted to Patrick's conversion as a youth while in slavery in Ireland. He is better on Patrick's Latin than he is on Patrick's religion. The difficulty of studying the life of Patrick for someone who insisted on the virtues of scientific history may have formed part of the attraction of the subject: could his kind of history handle a topic as difficult as the life of St Patrick? He explained the character of his approach: Todd had combined in one text critical discussions of the evidence and an account of Patrick's life. Bury would do something different: he would relegate scientific or critical history to the long series of appendices (together with the articles he had already published). 'These appendices', he wrote in the preface, 'belong to the science of history; the text is an effort in the art of historiography'.

A particular difficulty with which he wrestled in both text and appendices is that the deeds of Patrick are rarely revealed in the saint's own writings; for them Bury had to have recourse to much later sources, principally the works of two late seventh-century writers, Tírechán and Muirchú. Any attentive reader will notice the problems this caused. Whenever he is concerned with Patrick's activities rather than the general context, Bury's text is peppered with such phrases as 'according to ancient tradition', 'we may believe that', 'it seems that', 'the tale tells' and, above all, the single word 'may'. All these are signs that Bury is relying on evidence about 200 years later than Patrick. He argued that behind

Tírechán and Muirchú lay earlier sources in Irish, but it was very hard to show how old these sources might be or how much of Patrick's career was covered by them. Later scholars have, on the whole, considered it too risky to build a narrative on such conjectures.

The uncertain link between Patrick in the fifth century and Tírechán and Muirchú in the late seventh century was the weak point that was split apart by a book-length article in 1962 by the leading historian of early medieval Ireland at the time, D. A. Binchy. Bury was not the principal immediate target of Binchy's attack; instead his onslaught was focused on those who defended something like Bury's Patrick against an earlier critique by T. F. O'Rahilly. Binchy's article belongs fair and square in the tradition of Bury's scientific and critical history, and he was as firm in refusing to form any final judgement between Bury's defenders and his critics as was Bury himself on the controversies between the Protestant and Catholic divines. The effect of Binchy's article was profound: no reputable later scholar has thought it proper to use later evidence in the way Bury used it. A more recent ancient historian, E. A. Thompson, used his close and wide knowledge of Late Antiquity and a detailed exegesis of Patrick's own writings to develop a cautious picture of the saint's career. He kept clear of later evidence.

The change in the whole tendency of Patrician scholarship brought about by Binchy should not prevent recognition of the many particular good points of Bury's *Life*, quite apart from his broad understanding of the significance of Patrick in the history of Europe. He recognized clearly that Patrick's *Confessio* demonstrates beyond any practical doubt that, when Patrick served as a slave in Ireland in his youth, he did so near a forest in what is now Co. Mayo. Moreover, his subsequent mission to the Irish was in large part one directed to the people of that same district. Yet, it is the united testimony of the later sources that Patrick was a slave in Co. Antrim, in the valley of the Braid. This contrast is all the more odd because Tírechán was a native of the same district of Co. Mayo, and yet he accepted that Patrick was a slave in Ulster. Bury, therefore, could reject *in toto* a later tradition when he saw that it conflicted with fifth-century evidence.

One category of evidence that escaped unduly lightly from Bury's critical analysis of the sources was the annals. Where this became crucial was in the relationship between Patrick and Palladius. For the Irish chroniclers the starting point of the conversion was provided by an annal in one of their continental sources: the contemporary chronicle of Prosper of Aquitaine recorded that, in 431, Pope Celestine consecrated the deacon Palladius and sent him as bishop to the Irish that believed in Christ. The Irish chroniclers then placed Patrick's arrival as a missionary in the very next year. This dating fits a central point about Palladius and Patrick in the later sources: for them, Palladius only remained active in Ireland for a brief period, after which he left the island and died among the Britons or the Picts. The role of Palladius was transmuted into a mere chronological anchor for the far longer and more glorious career of Patrick together with a statement that papal authority lay at the beginning of organised Irish Christianity. Moreover, the Irish chroniclers faced a huge difficulty. They were concerned with the triumph of the sons of Niall in the northern half of Ireland. This triumph extended into the early sixth century; yet they had one of Niall's sons, Lóegaire, ruling at Tara when Patrick arrived, the better part of a century earlier, in 432. This makes it probable that their chronology was based on shifting Lóegaire backwards in time towards the annal recording the mission of Palladius. When one notes that Patrick's lifetime in these same sources is similarly elongated, so that his main obit was placed in 493, more than 60 years after his supposed arrival in 432, it becomes hard to resist the conclusion that the mission of Palladius was curtailed and Patrick's was placed earlier and elongated as parts of a single attempt to minimise Palladius and exalt Patrick. Todd had seen this in 1864, but it was resisted by Bury in 1905.

In the history of Patrician scholarship Bury's *Life* occupies an honourable place, above all because he could see where St Patrick belonged in the broad sweep of history. For that reason alone it remains an important text for modern scholars. Bury also made major contributions to the study of the later sources, which remain valuable for those who would place them where they belong, in the history of Ireland from the late seventh century onwards. There remain odd details in the writings of Tírechán and Muirchú that may descend from the fifth century, but we are hard put to it to define just what they are, and they do not include their broad conception of the career of the apostle of the Irish.

Thomas Charles-Edwards

PREFACE

PERHAPS the scope of this book will be best understood if I explain that the subject attracted my attention, not as an important crisis in the history of Ireland, but, in the first place, as an appendix to the history of the Roman Empire, illustrating the emanations of its influence beyond its own frontiers; and, in the second place, as a notable episode in the series of conversions which spread over northern Europe the religion which prevails to-day. Studying the work of the Slavonic apostles, Cyril and Methodius, I was led to compare them with other European missionaries, Wulfilas, for instance, and Augustine, Boniface, and Otto of Bamberg. When I came to Patrick, I found it impossible to gain any clear conception of the man and his work. The subject was wrapt in obscurity, and this obscurity was encircled by an atmosphere of controversy and conjecture. Doubts of the very existence of St Patrick had been entertained, and other views almost amounted to the thesis that if he did exist, he was not himself, but a namesake. It was at once evident that the material had never been critically sifted, and that it would be necessary to begin at the beginning, almost as if nothing had been done, in a field where much had been written.

This may seem unfair to the work of Todd, which in learning and critical acumen stands out pre-eminent from the mass of historical literature which has gathered round St Patrick. And I should like unreservedly to acknowledge that I found it an excellent introduction to the subject. But it left me doubtful about every fact connected with Patrick's life. The radical vice of the book is that the indispensable substructure is lacking. The preliminary task of criticising the sources methodically had never been performed. Todd showed his scholarship and historical insight in dealing with this particular passage or that particular statement, but such sporadic criticism was no substitute for methodical *Quellenkritik*. Hence his results might be right or wrong, but they could not be convincing.

It is a minor defect in Todd's *St Patrick* that he is not impartial. By this I mean that he wrote with an unmistakable ecclesiastical bias. It is not Implied that he would have ever stooped to a misrepresentation of the evidence for the purpose of proving a particular thesis. No reader would accuse him of that. But it is clear that he was anxious to establish a particular thesis. He does not conceal that the conclusions to which the evidence, as he interpreted it, conducted him were conclusions which he wished to reach. In other words, he approached a historical problem, with a distinct preference for one solution rather than another; and this preference was due to an interest totally irrelevant to mere historical truth. The business of a historian is to ascertain facts. There is something essentially absurd in his wishing that any alleged fact should turn out to be true or should turn out to be false. So far as he entertains a wish of the kind, his attitude is not critical.

The justification of the present biography is that it rests upon a methodical examination of the sources, and that the conclusions, whether right or wrong, were reached without any prepossession. For one whose interest in the subject is purely intellectual, it was a matter of unmixed indifference what answer might be found to any one of the vexed questions. I will not anticipate my conclusions here, but I may say that they tend to show that the Roman Catholic conception of St Patrick's work is, generally, nearer to historical fact than the views of some anti-Papal divines.

The fragmentary material, presenting endless difficulties and problems, might have been treated with much less trouble to myself if I had been content to weave, as Todd has done, technical discussions into the story. It was less easy to do what I have attempted, to cast matter of this kind into the literary shape of a biography—a choice which necessitated long appendices supplying the justifications and groundwork. These appendices represent the work which belongs to the science of history; the text is an effort in the art of historiography.[1]

It should be needless to say that, in dealing with such fragmentary material, reconstructions and hypotheses are inevitable. In ancient and mediæval history, as in physical science, hypotheses, founded on a critical examination of the data, are necessary for the advancement of knowledge. The reconstructions may fall to-morrow, but, if they are legitimate, they will not have been useless.

The future historian of Ireland will have much to discover about the political and social state of the island, which is still but vaguely understood, and the religion of the Scots, about which it may be affirmed that we know little more than nothing. These subjects await systematic investigation, and I have only attempted a slight sketch (Chapter IV.), confining myself to what it seemed possible to say with tolerable safety on the chief points immediately relevant to the scope of this monograph. But, notwithstanding the dimness of the background, I venture to hope that some new light has been thrown on the foreground, and that this study will supply a firmer basis for the life and work of Patrick, even if some of the superstructures should fall.

The two maps are merely intended to help the reader to see the whereabouts of some places which he might not easily find without reference to the Ordnance Survey. I consulted Mr. Orpen's valuable map of Early Ireland (unfortunately on a small scale) in Poole's *Historical Atlas of Modern Europe*. But he has used material which applies to a later period, and I have not ventured to follow him, for instance, in marking the boundary between the northern frontiers of the kingdoms of Connaught and Meath.

It was fortunate for me that my friend Professor Gwynn was engaged at the same time on a "diplomatic" edition of the records contained in the *Codex Armachanus,* which constitute the principal body of evidence. With a generosity which has placed me under a deep obligation, he put the results of his labour on the difficult text at my disposal, and I have had the invaluable help and stimulus of constant communication with him on many critical problems arising out of the text of the documents.

Since the book was in type I have received some communications from my friend Professor Rhŷs which suggest a hope that the mysterious Ban-nauenta, St Patrick's home, may perhaps be identified at last. I had conjectured that it should be sought near the Severn or the Bristol Channel. The existence of three places named Banwen (which may represent Bannauenta) in Glamorganshire opens a prospect that the solution may possibly lie there.

J. B. BURY.

SHORT BIBLIOGRAPHY

J. B. Bury on St Patrick

Bury, J. B., 'The Tradition of Muirchu's Text', *Hermathena*, 28 (1902), 172–207.

——'Tírechán's Memoir of St. Patrick', *English Historical Review*, 17 (1902), 235–67.

——'Supplementary Notes', ibid. 700–4.

——'Itinerary of Patrick in Connaught', *Proceedings of the Royal Irish Academy*, 24 C (1903), 153–68.

—— 'Sources of the Early Patrician Documents', *English Historical Review*, 19 (1904), 493–503.

—— *The Life of St. Patrick and His Place in History* (London, 1905).

Sources

Patrick, *Libri Epistolarum* (incl. the *Confessio* and the *Epistola ad Milites Corotici*), ed. L. Bieler, *Libri Epistolarum Sancti Patricii Episcopi*, 2 vols. (Irish Manuscripts Commission; Dublin, 1952; repr. Dublin, 1993).

Ed. and trans. R. P. C. Hanson with C. Blanc, *Saint Patrick: Confession et lettre à Coroticus*, Sources Chrétiennes 249 (Paris, 1978).

Ed. and trans. D. R. Howlett, *The Book of Letters of Saint Patrick the Bishop* (Blackrock, Co. Dublin, 1994).

English translations: L. Bieler, *The Works of St Patrick*, Ancient Christian Writers, 17 (London, 1963); R. P. C. Hanson, *The Life and Writings of the Historical Saint Patrick* (New York, 1983); D. Conneely, *The Letters of St Patrick* (Maynooth, 1993); T. O'Loughlin, *Saint Patrick: The Man and His Works* (London, 1999). This has a full bibliography.

Later sources

The Patrician Texts in the Book of Armagh, ed. and trans. L. Bieler,
Scriptores Latini Hiberniae, 10 (Dublin, 1979).
Bury had access to an early version of J. Gwynn, *Liber Ardmachanus.
The Book of Armagh* (Dublin, 1913). Cf. Bury, *Life*, p. x. This
remains standard.

Select secondary works on St Patrick

Binchy, D. A., 'Patrick and His Biographers: Ancient and Modern',
Studia Hibernica, 2 (1962), 7–173.
Hanson, R. P. C., *St Patrick, His Origins and Career* (Oxford, 1968).
Malaspina, E., *Patrizio e l'acculturazione latina dell' Irlanda* (Rome,
1985).
Thompson, E. A., *Who Was Saint Patrick?* (Woodbridge, 1985).

More general background

Charles-Edwards, T. M., *Early Christian Ireland* (Cambridge, 2000).
Ó Cróinín, D., *Early Medieval Ireland, 400–1200* (London, 1995).

On J. B. Bury

Whitby, M., 'Bury, John Bagnell (1861–1927)', *Oxford Dictionary of
National Biography* (Oxford, 2004); http://www.oxforddnb.com/
view/article/32202

I

ON THE DIFFUSION OF CHRISTIANITY BEYOND
THE ROMAN EMPIRE

THE series of movements and wanderings, settlements and conquests, which may be most fitly described as the expansion of the German and Slavonic races, began in the second century A.D., and continued for well - nigh a thousand years, reshaping the political geography and changing the ethnical character of Europe. The latest stage in the process was the expansion of the northern Germans of Scandinavia and Denmark, which led to the settlements of the Vikings and Danes in the west and to the creation of the Russian State by Swedes in the east. The general movement of European history is not grasped if we fail to recognise that the invasions and conquests of the Norsemen which began towards the close of the eighth century are the continuation of the earlier German expansion which we are accustomed to designate as the Wandering of the Peoples. It was not till this last stage that Ireland came within range of this general transformation, when, in the ninth century, Teutonic settlements were made on her coasts and a Teutonic kingdom was formed within her borders. Till then she had escaped the stress of the political vicissitudes of Europe. But, four centuries before, a force of another kind had drawn her into union with the continent and made her a part of the Roman world, so far as

the Roman world represented Christendom. Remaining still
politically aloof, still impervious to the influence of higher
social organisation, the island was swept into the spiritual
federation, which, through the act of Constantine, had become closely identified with the Roman State. This was what
the Roman Empire did for Ireland, not directly or designedly,
but automatically, one might say, through the circumstances
of its geographical position. The foundation of a church in
Ireland was not accomplished till the very hour when the
Empire was beginning to fall gradually asunder in the west;
and so it happens that when Europe, in the fifth century, is
acquiring a new form and feature, the establishment of the
Christian faith in the outlying island appears as a distinct,
though modest, part of the general transformation. *Ab in-
tegro saeclorum nascitur ordo,* and Ireland, too, has its small
place in the great change.

To understand the conversion of Ireland, which we are
here considering as an episode in the history of Europe, we
must glance at the general conditions of the early propagation
of the Christian idea. It would not be easy to determine
how much Christianity owes to the Roman Empire, and
we can hardly imagine what the rate and the mode of its
progress through southern and western Europe would have
been if these lands had not been united and organised by the
might of Rome. It is perhaps not an exaggeration to say that
the existence of the Empire was a condition of the success
of a universal religion in Europe; and it is assuredly true
that the hindrances which the Roman Government, for two
centuries and a half, opposed to its diffusion, by treating it
as the one foreign religion which could not be tolerated by

the State, were more than compensated by the facilities of steady and safe intercourse and communication, which not only helped the new idea to travel, but enabled its preachers and adherents to organise their work and keep in constant touch with one another.

The manner in which this faith spread in the west, and the steps in its progress, are entirely hidden from us; we can only mark, in a general way, some stages in the process.[1] We know that there were organised communities in Gaul in the second century, and organised communities in Britain at the end of the third; but in neither of these countries, it would seem, did the religion begin to spread widely till after its official recognition by the Emperor Constantine. At the end of the fourth century there were still large districts in Gaul, especially in the Belgic provinces, which were entirely heathen. In this respect Gaul and Britain present a notable contrast to the other great Atlantic country of the Empire. In the Spanish peninsula Christianity made such rapid strides, and the Spaniards adapted it so skilfully to their pagan habits, that before the time of Constantine Spain had become, throughout its length and breadth, a Christian land.

It could not be expected that, while there were still within the Roman frontiers many outlying districts where the new religion had not penetrated, the western churches could conceive the design of making any systematic attempt to convert the folks who lived beyond the borders of the Empire. The first duty of the bishops of Gaul and the bishops of Britain, if they undertook any missionary work, was to extend their faith in the still heathen parts of their own provinces. The single conspicuous case in which it reached a northern people,

independent of the Empire, is significant, for it exhibits the
kind of circumstances which helped this religion to travel.
The conversion of the West Goths in Dacia was not inaugurated by any missionary zeal on the part of the Church,
but came to pass through the means of Christian captives
whom the people had carried off in their invasions of Asia
Minor in the middle of the third century. The "apostle"
Wulfilas, whose work led to the general conversion of the
Goths, sprang from a Cappadocian family which had thus
been led into captivity, and had lived for two generations
in Gothic land. Gothic in spirit and sentiment, as he was
Gothic in name, he devoted himself to spreading the gospel
of the Christians among his people. His work was recognised and supported at Constantinople, but the fact remains
that the conversion of the Goths was due to the hostilities
which had brought Christian captives to their land, and not
to missionary enterprise of the Church. The part which captives played in diffusing a knowledge of their religion is, in
this instance, strikingly exemplified. The conversion of the
kingdom of Iberia under Mount Caucasus is another case.
The story that it became Christian in the reign of Constantine through the bond-slave Nino, who is still revered
there as the "enlightener and apostle of Georgia," rests upon
evidence only two generations later, and must have a foundation in fact.[2] And even if the tale is not accepted literally,
its existence illustrates the important part which Christian
captives played in the diffusion of their creed. This is expressly observed by the author of the treatise *On the Calling
of the Gentiles*. "Sons of the Church led captive by enemies
made their masters serve the gospel of Christ, and taught

the faith to those to whom the fortune of war had enslaved them."[3]

The same nameless writer, who composed his work in the fifth century, notices another channel by which knowledge of his religion was conveyed to the barbarians. Foreign soldiers, who enlisted in the army of the Empire, sometimes came under Christian influences in their garrison stations, and when they returned to their own homes beyond the Imperial frontier they carried the faith with them.[4]

That the silent and constant intercourse of commerce was also a means of propagation beyond the limits of the Empire cannot be doubted, though commercial relations and conditions in ancient and mediaeval history are among the hardest to realise because ancient and mediaeval writers never thought of describing them. The foundation of the Abyssinian church, however, exhibits the part which merchants, as well as the part which captives, might take in propagating a religious faith; and fortunately we possess an account which was derived directly from one of the captives who was concerned in the matter.[5]

A party of Greek explorers who had been sailing in southern seas landed on the coast of Abyssinia and were slaughtered by the natives, with the exception of two youths, who were spared to become slaves of the king. One served him as cup-bearer, the other, whose name was Frumentius, as secretary; and after the king's death his son's education was entrusted to these two men. Frumentius used his influence to help the Roman merchants who traded with Abyssinia to found a Christian church. He was afterwards permitted to return to his own country, but he resolved to dedicate his life to the propagation of Christianity in Abyssinia, and having been consecrated by Athanasius at Alexandria as Bishop of Axum, the Abyssinian capital town, he returned thither to foster the new church.

This course of events illustrates both the way in which captives helped to spread Christianity abroad, and also how the intercourse of trade could lead to the planting of Christian communities in lands outside the Empire. It illustrates the fact that up to the sixth century the extension of that faith to the barbarians was not due to direct efforts or deliberate design on the part of the Church, but to chapters of accidents which arose through the relations, hostile and pacific, of the Empire with its neighbours. The "mission" to the Gentiles was, in practice, limited by the Church to the Roman world, though the heads of the Church were always ready to recognise, welcome, and affiliate Christian communities which might be planted on barbarian ground by the accidents of private enterprise.

It was only after the Roman Empire had become officially Christian through the memorable decision of Constantine, that the conversion of neighbouring states (with the striking exception of Armenia)[6] really began; just after that change the victorious religion began to spread generally in Gaul and Britain. The work of Frumentius and the work of Wulfilas were alike subsequent to the revolution of Constantine. It would be difficult to estimate how great was the impetus which this religion derived, for the acceleration of its progress, from its acceptance by the head of the Roman State. But while it is evident that the Church gained immeasurably within the Empire by her sudden exaltation, it is perhaps generally overlooked how her changed position aided Christianity to pass out beyond the Empire's borders. We touch here on a fact of supreme importance—not less important, but more likely to escape notice, because it cannot be stated in terms, of definite occurrences:—the enormous prestige which the Roman Empire possessed in the minds of the barbarian peoples who dwelt beyond it. The observant student who follows with care the history of the expansion of Germany and the strange process by which the German kingdoms were established within the Empire in western Europe, is struck at every step by the profound respect which the barbarians evinced for the Empire and the Roman name throughout all their hostilities and injuries. While they were unconsciously dismembering it, they believed in its impregnable stability; Europe without the Empire was unimaginable; the dominion of Rome seemed to them part of the universal order, as eternal as the great globe itself. If we take into account this immeasurable reverence for Rome, which is one of the governing psychical facts in the history of the "wandering of the nations," we can discern what prestige a religion would acquire for neighbouring peoples when it became the religion of the Roman people and the Roman State. We can understand with what different eyes the barbarians must have regarded Christianity when it was a forbidden and persecuted doctrine and when it was raised to be a State religion. It at once acquired a claim on their attention; it was no longer merely one among many rival doctrines current in the Empire. Considerations of political advantage came in; and political motives could sway barbarians, no less than Constantine himself, in

determining their attitude to a religious creed. And the fact
that the Christian God was the God of that great Empire was
in itself a persuasive argument in his favour. Could a people
find any more powerful protector than the Deity who was
worshipped and feared by the greatest "nation" on earth? So
it seemed to the Burgundians, who embraced the Roman
religion, we are told,[7] because they conceived that "the God
of the Romans is a strong helper to those who fear Him."
The simple barbarians did not reason too curiously. It did
not occur to them that the Eternal City had achieved her
greatness and built her empire under the auspices of Jupiter
and Mars. There can be little doubt that, if the step taken
by Constantine had been postponed for a hundred years,
we should not find the Goths and the Vandals professing
Christianity at the beginning of the fifth century.

Among the independent neighbours of the Roman Empire, Ireland occupies a singular place as the only part of the
Celtic world which had not been gathered under the sceptre
of Rome.[8] It may be suspected that an erroneous opinion is
prevalent, just because it lay outside the Empire, that this
outlying island was in early times more separate and aloof
from Europe than its geographical position would lead us to
suppose. The truth is that we have but lately begun to realise
the frequency and prevalence of intercourse by sea before
historical records begin. It has been but recently brought
home to us that hundreds and hundreds of years before the
Homeric poems were created, the lands of the Mediterranean
were bound together by maritime communication. The same
thing is true of the northern seas at a later period. It is absurd
to suppose that the Celtic conquerors of Britain and of Iverne

burned their ships when they had reached the island shores and cut themselves off from intercourse with the mainland from which they had crossed. And we may be sure that it was not they who first established regular communications. We may be sure that the pre-Celtic peoples of south Britain and the Ivernians, who gave its name to Ireland, knew the waterways to the coasts of the continent. The intimate connexion of the Celts of Britain with their kinsfolk across the Channel is amply attested in Caesar's history of the conquest of Gaul; and in the ordinary histories of Britain the political connexion, which even took the shape of a Gallo-British kingdom, has hardly been duly emphasised. Ireland was further, but not far. Constant relations between this island and Britain were inevitable through mere proximity, but there is no doubt that regular communication was also maintained with Gaul[9] and with Spain. Whatever weight may be allowed to the Irish semi-mythical traditions which point to ancient bonds between Ireland and Spain—and in judging them we must remember that the Ivernians are of the same Mediterranean race as the Iberians—it is, for the Celtic period, highly significant to find Roman geographers regarding Ireland as midway between Spain and Britain,[10] a conception which seems to point unmistakably to direct intercourse between Irish and Spanish ports. But the trade of Ireland with the Empire is noticed by Tacitus,[11] and is illustrated by the knowledge which Romans could acquire of its geography. Ptolemy, in the second century, gives an account of the island, which, disfigured though it is, and in many parts undecipherable through the corruption of the place-names, can be tested sufficiently to show that it is based upon genuine information.

It does not surprise us that in our Roman records we hear no syllable of any relations with Ireland, when we remember how meagre and sporadic are the literary records of Roman rule in Britain from the time of Domitian to the premature close. We know, indeed, that at the very outset the question had been considered whether Ireland should be occupied or not. A general of Domitian thought the conquest ought to be attempted, but the government decided against his opinion.[12] The question has been asked why the Romans never annexed it? The answer is simple. After the time of Augustus no additions were made to Roman dominion except under the stress of political necessity. Britain was annexed by the generals of Claudius for the same reason which prompted Julius to invade it,—political necessity, arising from the dangerously close bonds which united the Britons with the Gauls. The inference is that in the case of Ireland there was no such pressing political necessity. The Goidels of Ireland were a different branch of the Celtic race, and the Britons could find in Ireland no such support as the Gauls found in Britain. This explanation accords with the fact that till the middle of the fourth century the Irish or Scots are not named among the dangerous invaders of the British province; they are not named at all.

But it would be a false inference from this silence to suppose that the government in Britain had not to take political account of their western neighbours. Ireland was well on the horizon of the Roman governors, and Irish affairs must from time to time have claimed their attention. The exile, of whom Agricola made much, was not, we might surmise, the last Irish prince who sought in Britain a refuge from enemies at home. But one important measure of policy has escaped oblivion, though not through Roman records. In the third century, it would seem, an Irish tribe which dwelled in the kingdom of Meath was driven from its land. The name of this tribe, the Dessi, still lives in their ancient home—the district of Deece.[13] Some of them migrated southward to the lands of the Suir and the Blackwater, where their name likewise survives in the districts of Decies.[14] But others sought new abodes beyond the sea, and they settled largely in South Wales. The migration of the Dessi rests on the records of Irish tradition, but it is confirmed by the clear evidence of inscribed stones which attest the presence of a Goidelic population in south-western Britain. Here we have to do with an act of policy on the part of the Roman Government similar to the policy pursued in other parts of the Empire. A foreign people was allowed to settle, perhaps under certain conditions of military service, on the south-western sea-board. Nor need these Goidelic settlers have consisted only of the Dessi, or the settlements have all been made at one time, and there seem to have been other settlements in Somerset, Devonshire, and Cornwall.

General considerations, then, supported by particular fragments of evidence which exist, would prepare us to learn, as something not surprising, but rather to be expected, that, by the end of the fourth century, Christians, and some knowledge of the Christian worship, should have found their way to the Irish shores. Beyond the regular intercourse with Britain, Gaul, and Spain there was the special circumstances of the Irish settlements in south-west Britain—a highroad for the new creed to travel;[15] and the great invasion in the middle of the fourth century, which will be mentioned in the next chapter, must have conveyed Christian captives to Ireland. In the conversion of this island, as elsewhere, captives played the part of missionaries. It will not then amaze us to find, when we reach the fifth century, that men go forth from Ireland to be trained in the Christian theology. It will not astonish us to learn that Christian communities exist which are ripe for organisation, or to find this religion penetrating into the house of the High Kings. We shall see reasons for supposing that the Latin alphabet had already made its way to Ireland,[16] and the reception of an alphabet generally means the reception of other influences from the same source.[17] For the present it is enough to have brought the relations of the Empire to Ireland somewhat into line with its relations to other independent neighbours.

II

THE CAPTIVITY AND ESCAPE OF PATRICK

§1. *Parentage and Capture*

THE conversion of Ireland to Christianity has, as we have seen, its modest place among those manifold changes by which a new Europe was being formed in the fifth century. The beginnings of the work had been noiseless and dateless, due to the play of accident and the obscure zeal of nameless pioneers; but it was organised and established, so that it could never be undone, mainly by the efforts of one man, a Roman citizen of Britain, who devoted his life to the task.

The child who was destined to play this part in the shaping of a new Europe was born before the close of the fourth century, perhaps in the year 389 A.D. His father, Calpurnius, was a Briton; like all free subjects of the Empire, he was a Roman citizen; and, like his father Potitus before him, he bore a Roman name. He belonged to the middle class of landed proprietors, and was a decurion or member of the municipal council of a Roman town. His home was in a village named Bannaventa, but we cannot with any certainty identify its locality. The only Bannaventa that we know lay near Daventry, but this position does not agree with an ancient indication that the village of Calpurnius was close to the western sea. As the two elements of the name Bannaventa were probably not uncommon in British geographical nomenclature, it is not a rash assumption that there were other small places so called besides the only Bannaventa which happens to appear in Roman geographical sources, and we may be inclined to look for the Bannaventa of Calpurnius in south-western Britain, perhaps in the regions of the lower Severn. The village must have been in the neighbourhood of a town possessing a municipal council of decurions, to which Calpurnius belonged. It would not be right to infer that it was a town with the rank of a *colonia,* like Gloucester, or of a *municipium,* like St. Albans; for smaller Roman towns, such as were technically known as *praefecturae, fora,* and *conciliabula,* might be managed by municipal councils.

To be a decurion, or member of the governing council, of a Roman town in the days of Calpurnius and his father was, throughout the greater part of the Roman dominion, an unenvied dignity. Every landowner in a municipality who did not belong to the senatorial class was obliged to be a decurion, provided he possessed sixteen acres or upwards; and on these landowners the chief burden of imperial taxation fell. They were in this sense "the sinews of the republic." They were bound to deliver to the officials of the imperial treasury the amount of taxation levied upon their community; it was their duty both to collect the tax and to assess the proportion payable by the individual proprietor. In the fourth century, while the class of great landed proprietors, who were mainly senators and entirely free from municipal obligations, was increasing, the class of small landowners

diminished in numbers and declined in prosperity. This decline progressed rapidly, and the imperial laws which sought
to arrest it suggest an appalling picture of economic decay
and hopeless misery throughout the provinces. The evils of
perverse legislation were aggravated by the corruption and
tyranny of the treasury officials, which the Emperors, with
the best purposes, seemed powerless to prevent. Men devised
and sought all possible means of escaping from the sad fate
of a decurion's dignity. Many a harassed taxpayer abandoned
his land, surrendered his freedom, and became a labourer
on the estate of a rich landlord to escape the miseries of
a decayed decurion's life. We find the Emperor Maxentius
punishing Christians by promoting them to the dignity of a
decurion.

It is unknown to us whether the municipal classes in
Britain suffered as cruelly as their brethren in other parts
of the Empire. The history of this island throughout the
last century of Roman rule is almost a blank. It would be
hazardous to draw any inferences from the agricultural prosperity of Britain, whose corn-fields, notwithstanding the fact
that large tracts of land which is now under tillage were then
woodland, sometimes supplied the Roman legions on the
Rhine with their daily bread. But it is possible, for all we
know, that members of the British municipalities may have
enjoyed a less dreary lot than the downtrodden decurions of
other provinces.

There was one class of decurions which seems to have
caused the Emperors considerable perplexity. It was those
who, whether from a genuine religious motive or in order
to shirk the municipal burdens, took orders in the Christian

Church. A pagan Emperor like Julian had no scruple in re-calling them sternly to their civil duties, but Christian Em-perors found it difficult to assert such a principle. They had to sustain the curial system at all costs, and yet avoid giving offence to the Church. Theodosius the Great laid down that the estates of decurions who had become presbyters or dea-cons before a certain year should be exempt from municipal obligations, but that those who had taken orders after that year should forfeit their lands to the State. He qualified this law, however, by a later enactment, which provided that if the presbyter or deacon had a son who was not in orders, the son might keep the paternal property and perform the accompanying duties.

Now Calpurnius belonged to this class of decurions who had sought ordination. He was a Christian deacon, and his father before him had been a Christian presbyter. And it would seem as if they had found it feasible to combine their spiritual with their worldly duties. In any case, we may assume that the property remained in the family; it was not forfeited to the State.

Whether the burdens laid upon them from Milan or Con-stantinople were heavy or light, Calpurnius and his fellows in the northern island were keenly conscious that the rule of their Roman lords had its compensations. For Britain was beset by three bold and ruthless foes. The northern frontier of the province was ever threatened by the Picts of Caledonia. Her western shores dreaded the descents of the Gaels and Scots of Ireland, while the south and east were exposed to those Saxon freebooters who were ultimately to conquer the island. Against these enemies, ever watching for a favourable opportunity to spoil their rich neighbour, the Roman garrison was usually a strong and sure protection for the peaceful Britons. But favourable opportunities sometimes came. Potitus, at least, if not Calpurnius, must have shared in the agonies which Britain felt in those two terrible years when she was attacked on all sides, by Pict, by Scot, and by Saxon, when Theodosius, the great Emperor's father, had to come in haste and put forth all his strength to deliver the province from the barbarians. In the valley of the Severn the foes whom men had to dread now were Irish freebooters, and we need not doubt that in those years their pirate crafts sailed up the river and brought death and ruin to many. Theodosius defeated Saxon, Pict, and Scot, and it would seem that he pursued the Scots across the sea, driving them back to their own shores. The Court poet of his grandson sings how icebound Hiverne wept for the heaps of her slain children. After this, the land had peace for a space. Serious and thoroughgoing measures were taken for its defence, and an adequate army was left under a capable commander. Men could breathe freely once more. But the breathing space lasted less than fifteen years. The usurpation of the tyrant Maximus brought new calamities to Britain. Maximus assumed the purple (A.D. 383) by the will of the soldiers, who were ill-satisfied with the government of Gratian; and if the provincials approved of this rash act, they perhaps hoped that Maximus would be content with exercising authority in their own island. But even if Maximus did not desire a more spacious field for his ambition, such a course was perhaps impracticable. It would have been difficult for any usurper to maintain himself, with the adhesion

of Britain alone, against the power of the lord of the West.
Probably the best chance of success, the best chance of life,
for the tyrant lay in winning Gaul. And so Maximus crossed
the Channel, taking the army, or a part of it, with him.
His own safety was at stake; he recked not of the safety of the
province; and whatever forces he left on the shores and on
the northern frontier were unequal to the task of protecting
the island against the foes who were ever awaiting a pro-
pitious hour to pounce upon their prey. Bitterly were the
Britons destined to rue the day when Maximus was invested
with the purple. Denuded of defenders, they had again to
bear the inroads of Pict, Saxon, and Scot. Rescue came after
the fall of Maximus (A.D. 388), and the son of their former
defender, the Emperor Theodosius, empowered his most
trusted general, Stilicho, to make all needed provision for
the defence of the remote province. The enemies seem to
have escaped, safe and sated, from the shores of Britain before the return of the army; no fighting devolved on Stilicho;
he had only to see to works of fortification and defence.
But it was high time for legions to return; Britain, says a
contemporary poet, was well-nigh done to death.

The woes and distresses of these years must have been
witnessed and felt by Calpurnius and his household, and
they must have experienced profoundly the joy of relief when
their country was once more defended by an adequate army.
It was probably just before or just after this new period of
security had begun that a son was born to Calpurnius and
his wife Concessa. It may have been the habit of the native
provincials to give their children two names, a Latin name,
which stamped them as Romans, as well as a British name,

which would naturally be used in home life. Calpurnius called his son Patricius. But if Patricius talked as a child with his father and mother the Brythonic tongue of his forefathers, he bore the name of Sucat. He was thus double-named, like the Apostle Paul, who bore a Roman as well as a Jewish name from his youth up.[1] But another Roman name, Magonus, is also ascribed to Patrick; and possibly his full style—as it would appear in the town registry when he should come of age to exercise the rights of a citizen—was Patricius Magonus Sucatus. Such a name would be strictly analogous to that of a Roman historian of Gothic family who lived in a later generation, Renatus Profuturus Frigeridus.[2]

As the son of a deacon, Patrick was educated in the Christian faith, and was taught the Christian scriptures. And we may be sure that he was brought up to feel a deep reverence for the Empire in which he was born a freeman and citizen, and to regard Rome as the mighty bulwark of the world—

qua nihil in terris complectitur altius aether.

This feeling comes out in his writings; it may have been strengthened by the experiences of his life, but the idea must have been with him from his very cradle. Peaceful folk in Britain in those days could have imagined no more terrible disaster than to be sundered from the Empire; Rome was the symbol of peace and civilisation, and to Rome they passionately clung. The worst thing they had to dread from year to year was that the Roman army should be summoned to meet some sudden need in another province.

But as Patrick grew up, the waves were already gathering, to close slowly over the island, and to sweep the whole of western Europe. The great Theodosius died, and his two feeble successors slumbered at Milan and Constantinople, while along all the borders, or even pressing through the gates, were the barbarians, armed and ready, impressed by the majesty of Rome, but hungry for the spoils of the world. Hardly was Theodosius at rest in his tomb when Greece was laid waste by the Goths, and Athens trembled at the presence of Alaric. But men did not yet realise, even in their dreams, the strange things to come, whereof this was the menace and the presage. When the rumour of Alaric and his Goths reached the homesteads of Britain, it must have struck men's ears as a thing far off, a trouble in which they could have no part. And the danger that stole upon the Empire was muffled and disguised. Alaric was a Goth, but at the same time he was an imperial general, a Master of Soldiers, a servant of the Roman State, profoundly loyal to the Empire, the integrity of which he was undermining.

A few years later Britain was startled by sudden tidings. Alaric and his Goths had entered Italy itself; the Emperor Honorius was trembling on his throne, and the armies of the west must hasten to defend him. The message came from Stilicho, the general on whose strength and craft the safety of western Europe in these years depended, and one Britannic legion obeyed the summons to Italy. The islanders must again have been sick at heart in daily expectation of the assaults of their old enemies.

Those enemies were not asleep, and they rose up presently to take advantage of the favourable time. At this point we encounter an Irish king, whose name is famous in the obscure history of his own land. King Niall was the High-king of

Ireland in the days of the rebellion of Maximus, and may possibly have joined in the marauding expeditions which vexed Britain during those years. His deeds are enveloped in legend, but the exalted notion which his countrymen formed of his prowess is expressed in the vain tale that he invaded Gaul and conquered as far as the Alps. To the annals of the Empire king Niall is as unknown as the princelings of remotest Scythia, but in Britain his name must have been a familiar word. The tradition that he died out of his own country, but slain by the hand of a fellow-countryman, can hardly fail to be founded on fact; and when the Irish annals tell us that he met his death "by the Sea of Wight," there is nothing in the circumstances of the time which forbids us to believe the record. If the date assigned to his death, A.D. 405, is roughly correct, this last hosting of Niall was made before the Roman army had finally left the island, but during the disorders which preceded its departure.

It may have been at this crisis in the history of Britain that the event happened which shaped the whole life of the son of Calpurnius, who had now reached the age of sixteen, in his home near the western sea. A fleet of Irish freebooters came to the coasts or river-banks in the neighbourhood seeking plunder and loading their vessels with captives. Patrick was at his father's farmstead, and was one of the victims. Men-servants and maid-servants were taken, but his parents escaped; perhaps they were not there, or perhaps the pirates could not carry more than a certain number of slaves, and chose the young.

Thus was Patrick, in his seventeenth year, carried into captivity in Ireland—"to the ultimate places of the earth," as he says himself, as if Ireland were severed by half the globe from Britain. The phrase shows how thoroughly, how touchingly Roman was Patrick's geographical view. The Roman Empire was the world, and all outside its fringe was in darkness, the ultimate places of the earth.

§2. *Captivity and Escape*

Of all that befell Patrick during his captivity in Ireland we know little, yet the little knowledge we possess is more immediate and authentic than our acquaintance with any other episode of his life, because it comes from his own pen. But at the outset we encounter a puzzling contradiction between Patrick's own words and the tradition which was afterwards current in Ireland as to the place of his bondage.

When the boats of his captors reached their haven, Patrick was led—so we should conclude from his own story—across the island into the kingdom of Cannaught, to serve a master in the very furthest parts of the "ultimate land." His master dwelled near the wood of Fochlad, "nigh to the western sea," in north-western Connaught, to this day a wild and desolate land, though the forest has long since been cleared away. A part of this bleak country belonged to Amolngaid, who after-wards became king of Connaught, and it is still called by his name, Tir-awley, "the land of Amoln-gaid." But the wood of Fochlad was probably of larger extent than the district of Tirawley; it may have stretched over Mayo to the western promontory of Murrisk. Here, we should perhaps suppose, close to Crochan Aigli, the mount which has been immemorially associated with Patrick's name,[3] the British slave served his master for six years.

But our other records transport us to a distant part of Ireland, far away from the forest of Fochlad, to Pictish soil near the eastern coast of Ulster. Here in the lands east of Lough Neagh, the old race, driven eastward from central Ulster, still held out. The name Ulaid, which originally designated the whole of northern Ireland—even as now in its Danish form of Ulster—had come to be specially applied to the eastern corner, whither the true Ulidians had been driven. It seemed now to be the true Ulaid. Within the borders of Ulidia, in this restricted sense, there was a marked division. In the extreme north were the Scots, and in the south were the Picts. The small land of the Scots was known as Dal-riada, and the larger land of the Picts as Dal-aradia.[4] It is supposed that both peoples, those known as Scots and those known as Picts, represented the older races, which possessed Ireland before the coming of the Goidelic invaders, whose language ultimately prevailed throughout the whole island.

Here, it was believed and recorded, Patrick served a master whose name was Miliucc. His lands and his homestead were in northern Dalaradia, and Patrick herded his droves of pigs on Mount Miss. The name of this mountain still abides unchanged, though by coalescing with *sliabh*, the Gaelic word for "mountain," it is slightly disguised in the form Slemish. Not really lofty, and not visible at a distance of many miles, yet, when you come within its range, Mount Miss dominates the whole scene and produces the impression of a massive mountain. Its curious, striking shape, like an inverted bowl, round and wide-brimmed, exercises a sort of charm on the eye, and haunts one who is walking in the valley of the Braid, somewhat as the triangular form of Pentelicus, clear-cut like the pediment of a temple, follows one about in the plain of Athens.

It was in this valley of the Braid and on the slopes of Miss that, according to the common tradition and general belief, Patrick for six years did the bidding of his lord.[5] But it is certain, from his own words, that he served near the forest of Fochlad. An attempt may be made to reconcile the contradiction by assuming that he changed masters, and that, having dwelled at first in the west, he was sold to another master in Dalaradia; but his own description of his bond-age seems hardly compatible with such a conjecture. The simplest solution seems to be a frank rejection of the story which connected his captivity with Mount Miss in the land of the Picts.

While he ate the bitter bread of bondage in a foreign land, a profound spiritual change came over him. He had never given much thought to his religion, but now that he was a thrall amid strangers, "the Lord," he says, "opened the sense of my unbelief." The ardour of religious emotion, "the love and fear of God," so fully consumed his soul that in a single day or night he would offer a hundred prayers; and he describes himself, in woodland or on mountain-side, rising from his bed before dawn and going forth to pray in hail, or rain, or snow.

> His contemplation was above the earth,
> And fixed on spiritual object.

Thus the years of his bondage were also the years of his "conversion," and he looked back upon this stage in his spiritual development as the most important and critical in his life.

But he was homesick, and he was too young to abandon hope of deliverance and escape from the wild outland into which fate had cast him. He longed and hoped, and we may be sure that he prayed, to win his way back within the borders of the Roman Empire. His waking hopes came back to him at night as responsive voices in his dreams. He heard a voice that said to him in his sleep, "Thou doest well to fast; thou shalt soon return to thy native land." And another night it said, "Behold, thy ship is ready." Patrick took these dream-voices for divine intimations, and they heartened him to make an attempt to escape. Escape was not easy, and was beset with many perils. For the port where he might hope to find a foreign vessel was about a hundred and eighty miles from his master's house. Patrick, in describing his escape, does not name the port, but we may conjecture that it was Inver-dea, at the mouth of the stream, which is now called the Vartry, and reaches the sea near the town of Wicklow. The resolution of attempting this long flight, with the danger of falling into the hands of some other master, if not of being overtaken by his own, is ascribed by Patrick to the promptings of a higher will than his. He escaped all dangers and reached the port, where he knew no man. But at all events he had chosen the season of his flight well. The ship of his dreams was there, and was soon to sail. It was a ship of traders; their cargo was aboard, and part of the cargo consisted of dogs, probably Irish wolf-hounds. Patrick spoke to some of the crew, and made a proposal of service. He was willing to work his passage to the port to which the vessel was bound. The proposal seems to have been at first entertained, but afterwards the shipmaster objected, and said sharply, "Nay, in no wise shalt thou come with us." The disappointment, as safety seemed within grasp, must have been bitter, and Patrick turned away from the mariners to seek the lodging where he had found shelter. As he went he prayed, and before he finished his prayer he heard one of the crew shouting behind him, "Come quickly, for they are calling you." The shipmaster had been persuaded to forego his objections, and Patrick set sail from the shores of Ireland with this rough company.

To what country or race the crew belonged we are not told; we learn only that they were heathen. They wished to enter into some solemn compact of abiding friendship with Patrick, but he refused to be adopted by them. "I would not," he says, using a quaint phrase, "suck their breasts because of the fear of God. Nevertheless I hoped of them that they might come to the faith of Christ, for they were heathen, and therefore I held on with them."

They sailed for three days before they made land. The name of the coast which they reached is hidden from us, and there is something very strange about the whole story. The voyage was clearly uneventful. They were not driven by storm or stress of weather out of their course to some undesired shore. There is nothing in the tale, as Patrick tells it himself, to suggest that the ship did not reach the port to which it was bound. Yet when they landed, their way lay through a desert, and they journeyed through the desert for eight and twenty days in all. Their food ran short, and at last starvation threatened them; many of their dogs were exhausted and left to die on the wayside. Then the shipmaster said to Patrick, "Now, O Christian, thou sayest thy God is great and almighty. Why then dost thou not pray for us? For we are in danger of starvation, and there is no likelihood of our seeing any man." And Patrick, in the spirit of the missionary, replied, "Nothing is impossible to the Lord, my God. Turn to him truly, that he may send you food in your path this day till ye are filled, for he has plenty in all places." Presently a drove of pigs appeared on the road, and the starving wayfarers killed many, and rested there two nights, and were refreshed. They were as ready as Patrick himself to believe that the appearance of the swine was a miraculous answer to his prayer, and he won high esteem in their eyes.

As Patrick slept here, his body satisfied, after long privation, by a plenteous meal, he had a dream, which he remembered vividly as long as he lived. He dreamed that a great stone fell upon him, and that he could not move his limbs. Then he called upon Elias,[6] and the beams of the rising sun awoke him, and the feeling of heaviness fell away. Patrick regarded this nightmare as a temptation of Satan, and imagined that Christ had come to his aid. The incident has a ridiculous side, but it shows the intense religious excitement of Patrick at this period, ready to see in the most trivial occurrence a direct interposition from heaven; and we must remember how in those days dreams were universally invested with a certain mystery and dread.

For nine days more Patrick and his companions travelled through deserted places, but were not in want of food or shelter; on the tenth they came to the habitations of men. Patrick had no thoughts of remaining with them longer than he needed. He had heard in a dream a divine voice answering his thoughts and saying, "Thou shalt remain with them two months." This dream naturally guided him in choosing the time of his escape. At the end of two months he succeeded in releasing himself from his masters.

In his description of this strange adventure he leaves us to divine the geography as best we may, for he relates it as if it had happened in some nameless land beyond the borders of the known world. But the circumstances enable us to determine that the ship made for the coast of Gaul. It can be shown that its destination was not Britain, and Gaul is the only other land which could have been reached in three days or thereabouts. The aim of the traders with their Irish dogs must have been to reach southern Europe, and the place of disembarkation would naturally have been Nantes or Bordeaux. The story of the long faring through a wilderness might be taken to illustrate the condition of western and south-western Gaul at this period. For much about the time at which Patrick's adventures happened, Gallic poets were writing heartbreaking descriptions of the desolation which had been brought upon this country by the great invasion of Vandals and Sueves and other barbarous peoples. The Vandals and Sueves had indeed already left it to pass into Spain, but they had left it waste. Strong castles, walled cities, sings one poet, could not escape; the hands of the barbarians reached even lonely lodges in dismal wilds and the very caves in the hills. "If the whole ocean," cries another, "had poured its waters into the fields of Gaul, its vasty waves would have spared more than the invaders."

But even in the exceptional conditions of the time, it is surprising that a party, starting from a port on the west coast and travelling to the Mediterranean, should have walked for four weeks without seeing a human abode and in dire peril of starvation. We must suppose that they avoided, deliberately and carefully, beaten roads, and perhaps made considerable halts, in order to avoid encounters with roaming bands of the Teutonic barbarians.

Though Patrick did not mention the scene of his journey in the narrative which he left behind him, he used to tell his disciples how he had "the fear of God as a guide in his journey through Gaul and Italy." This confirms the conclusion, to which the other evidence points, that Gaul was the destination of the crew, and also intimates that he travelled with his companions through Gaul to Italy. It was in Italy, then, we must suppose, that he succeeded in escaping from them.

The book in which he described this episode was written by Patrick, as we shall see hereafter, when he was an old man. He rigidly omitted all details which did not bear upon his special purpose in writing it. The whole tale of his captivity and escape, undefined or vaguely defined by landmarks or seamarks, as if the places of the adventures had no name or lay beyond the range of all human charts, is designed to display exclusively the spiritual significance of those experiences. That the land of his captivity was Ireland, this was indeed significant; but otherwise names of men and places were of no concern and might be allowed to drop away. Patrick, in reviewing this critical period of his life, reproduces the select incidents as they impressed him at the moment, contributing, as he believed, to his own spiritual development, or illustrating the wonderful ways in which Heaven had dealt with him.

III

IN GAUL AND BRITAIN

§1. *At Lérins*

PATRICK has not told us where, or in what circumstances, he parted from his companions, nor has he
related his subsequent adventures. When he found himself
free his first thought would have been, we should suppose,
to make his way back to his home in Britain. We saw that he
probably succeeded in escaping from his fellow-travellers in
Italy, and his easiest way home might in that case have been
by the coast road through Liguria and Provence to Marseilles.
From whatever quarter he started, he seems to have reached
the coast of Provence. For here at length, amid perplexing,
broken clues, we have a definite trace of his path; here at
length we can fix an episode in his life to a small plot of
ground.

In the later part of the fourth century the influence of the
Eastern on the Western mind had displayed itself not only
in theological thought, but also in the spread of asceticism
and the foundation of monastic societies, especially through
the influence of men like Ambrose, Martin of Tours, and
Jerome. In choosing their lonely dwelling-places, the eyes of
anchorets did not overlook the little deserted islands which
lay here and there off the coast in the western Mediterranean.

Island cloisters studded the coast of Italy "like a necklace" before the end of the fourth century, and soon they began to appear off the coast of Provence. It was perhaps while Patrick was a slave in Ireland that a traveller, weary of the world, came back from the east to his native Gaul, and, seeking a spot where he might found a little society of monks who desired to live far from the turmoil of cities, he was directed to the uncouth islet of Lerinus, which no man tilled or approached because it was infested by snakes. Honoratus took possession of it and reclaimed it for cultivation. Wells were dug, and sweet water flowed "in the midst of the bitterness of the sea." Vines were planted and cells were built, and a little monastic community gathered round Honoratus, destined within a few years to be more illustrious than any of the older island cloisters. Lerinus is the outermost of the two islands which lie opposite to the cape of Cannes, smaller and lower than its fellow Lero, which screens it from view, bearing at the present day the name of the man who made it significant in history.[1] It is difficult to realise as one walks round it to-day and sees a few stones, relics of its ancient monks, that at one time it exercised a great if unobtrusive influence in southern Gaul. Its peaceful, sequestered cells, "withdrawn into the great sea," *in mare magnum recedentia,* had a wonderful attraction for men who had been shipwrecked in the tumbling world, or who desired unbroken hours for contemplation—*vacare et videre.*

Patrick found a refuge in the island cloister of Honoratus, and in that island we are for the first time treading ground where we have reason to think that he lived for a considerable time. We should like to know the circumstances of his admission to this community, but his own picture of the state of his mind enables us to understand how easily he could have been moved by the ascetic attractions of the monastery to interrupt his homeward journey and lead a religious life in the *sacrae solitudines* of Lerinus for a few years.

Among the men of some note who sojourned in the monastery in its early days was Hilary, who afterwards became Bishop of Arelate; Maximus, who was the second abbot, and then Bishop of Reii; Lupus, who subsequently held the see of Trecasses; Vincentius, who taught and wrote in the cloister; and Eucherius, who composed, among other works, a treatise in praise of the hermit's life. Eucherius had built a hut for himself and his wife Galla, aloof from the rest of the brotherhood, in the larger island of Lero. It was remembered how one day Honoratus sent a messenger across in a boat with a letter on a wax tablet, and Eucherius, seeing the abbot's writing, said, "To the wax you have restored its honey."

As the monastic spirit grew and spread, many a stranger set his face to Lerinus, hoping, as men hoped greatly in those days, that "he might break through the wall of the passions and ascend by violence to the kingdom of heaven." Among those who joined the new society was Faustus, a compatriot of Patrick. But it is unknown whether he was at Lérins at this time; perhaps he was still only a child, for we first hear of him in the abbotship of Maximus, who succeeded Honoratus,[2] and whom he himself was destined to succeed.[3] Faustus had enjoyed an education such as Patrick never acquired. He was a student of ancient philosophy, and a master of style, as style was then understood. He was afterwards the valued friend and correspondent of the greatest man of letters of that century, Sidonius Apollinaris. Crude and rustic must Patrick have seemed to his fellow-countryman, if they met at Lérins. Yet to-day the name of Faustus has passed out of men's memory, and Patrick's is familiar in the households of western Christendom, and in far-western Christendom beyond the ocean.

There can be no doubt that the years which he spent at Lérins exercised an abiding influence on Patrick. He was brought under the spell of the monastic ideal; and though his life was not to be sequestered, but out in the active world of men, monastic societies became a principal and indispensable element in his idea of a Christian Church. It is improbable that during these years of seclusion he was stirred, even faintly, by the idea of devoting himself to the work of spreading Christianity in the barbarous land associated with his slavery and shame. But he was profoundly convinced that during the years of his bondage he had been held as in the hollow of God's hand; whatever hopes or ambitions he may have cherished in his boyhood must have been driven from his heart by the stress of his experience, and in such a frame of mind the instinct of a man of that age was to turn to a religious life. At Lérins, perhaps, his desire, so far as he understood it, was to remain a monk; *uenire ad eremum summa perfectio est.* But there were energies and feelings in him which such a life would not have contented. At the end of a few years he left the monastery to visit his kinsfolk in Britain, and there he became conscious of the true destiny of his life.

§2. *At Home in Britain*

When Patrick returned to his old home, his kinsfolk welcomed him "as a son,"[4] and implored him to stay and not part from them again. But if he had any thought of yielding to their persuasions, it was dismissed when he became aware, all at once, that the aim of his life was determined. The idea of labouring among the heathen, which may have been gradually, though quite unconsciously, gathering force and secretly winning possession of his brain, suddenly stood full-grown, as it were, face to face with him in a sensible shape. In a vision of the night it seemed to him that he saw a man standing by his side. It was a certain Victoricus. We may suppose that Patrick had made this man's acquaintance in Gaul, and that he was interested in Ireland, but his only appearance in history is in Patrick's dream. To the dreamer he seemed to have come from Ireland, and in his hand he held a bundle of letters. "And he gave me one of these, and I read the beginning of the letter, which contained 'the voice of the Irish.' And as I read the beginning of it, I fancied that I heard the voice of the folk who were near the wood of Fochlad, nigh to the western sea. And this was the cry: 'We pray thee, holy youth, to come and again walk amongst us as before.' I was pierced to the heart and could read no more; and thereupon I awoke." This is the dreamer's description of his dream. But, as the story was told in later days, the cry that pierced his heart was uttered by the young children of Fochlad, even by the children still unborn. There is nothing of this in Patrick's words, yet the tradition betrays a true instinct of the significance of the dream. It brings out more intensely and pathetically how the forlorn condition of the helpless unbaptized, condemned to everlasting punishment by the doctrine of the Church, could appeal irresistibly to the pity of a Christian who held that rigorous doctrine.

This doctrine was closely connected with the question which, at this time, above all other questions, was agitating western Christendom; and, strange to say, the controversy had been opened by a man of Irish descent. It is possible that, as some claim, Pelagius was born in Ireland, but the evidence rather points to the conclusion that he belonged to an Irish family settled in western Britain. His name represents, doubtless, some Irish sea-name such as Muirchu, "hound of the sea." While Patrick was serving in Ireland, Pelagius was in Rome, thinking out one of the great problems which has constantly perplexed the meditations of men, and promulgating a view which arrested the interest or compelled the attention of leaders of theological opinion from York to Carthage, from Carthage to Jerusalem. For some years the Roman Empire echoed with his fame.

Pelagianism is not one of those dull, lifeless heresies which have no more interest than the fact that they once possessed for a short space the minds of men a long while dead. At this period the onward movement of human thought was confined within the lines of theology, couched in theological language, and we must distinguish those questions which, like the Arian and Pelagian, involve speculations of perpetual human interest from controversies which touch merely the formulae of a special theology. We need not enter upon the actual course of the debate in which Pelagius and Augustine represented two opposed tendencies of religious and philosophic thought, destined to reappear in the time of the Reformation, but we are concerned with the general significance of the questions involved. The chief and central principle of Pelagius was the recognition of freewill as an inalienable property of human nature. In every action a man is free to choose between good and evil, and his choice is not determined, and has not been predetermined, by the Deity who originally gave to man that power of choosing. Pelagius regarded freewill as the palladium and surrogate of the dignity of human nature. This view logically excluded the doctrine of original sin, inherited from Adam, as well as the doctrine of predestination; it implied that infants are born sinless, and that baptism is not necessary to save them from hell; it implied that it was perfectly possible, however difficult, for a man who had not embraced the Christian faith, or been bathed in the mystical waters of baptism, to lead a sinless life. It is clear that this thesis, as the opponents of Pelagius saw and said, struck at the very root of the theory of the "Atonement"—at least as the "Atonement" was crudely conceived by the Church in dependence on the old Jewish story of the fall of Adam. Pelagius does not seem to have succeeded in really working his theory of human nature into the Christian system, which he fully accepted, and this was the logical weakness of his position in the theological debate.

Pelagius was not a mere speculator. Himself a monk and rigorous liver, he had in view the practical aim of raising the morality of Christians, and his particular view of human nature and "sin" bore directly on this practical aim. For if the purpose of religion is to realise the ideal of holiness and draw men up, above the level of commonplace sensual life, to high and heavenly things, and if the doctrine of sin was framed by the Church with this view, it might well have seemed to an observer that there lay a practical danger in such a doctrine. There was a danger that, if men were taught that they were born evil and impotent to resist evil by efforts of their own nature, the moral consciousness would be stifled and paralysed by a belief so dishonouring to humanity. The assertion of the freedom of the will by Pelagius, and his denial of innate sin, represent a reaction of the moral consciousness against the dominance of the religious consciousness, and although he speaks within the Church, he is really asserting the man against the Christian, defending the honour of the "reasonable creature."[5]

To the surveyor of the history of humanity this is the interest which Pelagius possesses, an interest which is generally obscured in the dust of controversy. He was the champion of human nature as such, which the Christian Church, in pursuance of its high objects, dishonoured and branded as essentially depraved. He was the champion of all the good men who lived "on the ridge of the world," as men of his own race would have said, before ever Jesus was born, of all those whose minds were fixed on invisible things, of all the noble and sinless pagans, were they many or few. This was the merit of Pelagius, to have attempted to rescue the dignity of human nature oppressed by the doctrine of sin; and we who realise how much our race owes to the peoples of antiquity may feel particular sympathy with him who dared to say that, before Jesus, sinless men had lived upon earth.[6] Of few men have the Celts of Ireland or Britain better reason to be proud than of the bold thinker who went forth to speak holy words for humanity against the inhuman side of the Christian faith. He was ranged against the authorities of Augustine and Jerome, but he was not fond of fighting; he wished to keep the whole question out of the region of dogma, and let it remain a matter of opinion; he never sought to get his own views sanctioned by a council of the Church. But the strife and the defeat are of subordinate interest. What interests us is that Pelagius, himself originally stimulated by Rufinus, stimulated thinking men throughout the West, and induced many to modify their views about freewill and congenital sin.

The repose of Lérins was not uninvaded by the sounds of this debate, and some of its more notable monks showed hereafter that they had been profoundly influenced by the arguments of Pelagius. The subject therefore must have been familiar to Patrick, and the terrible doctrine, impugned by the Scottish heretic, that infants, being sinful at their birth, incur the everlasting punishment of the wicked until they are redeemed through the mysterious rite of baptism, might well affect his imagination. Nothing could have done more to quicken his concern for the unbaptized people by the western sea than a vivid realisation of this doctrine.

The self-revealing dream convinced Patrick that he was destined to go as missioner and helper to Ireland—*ad ultimum terrae,* to the limit of the world. Yet he felt hesitation and uncertainty, distrusting his own fitness for such an enterprise, conscious of the defective education of his youth; and he felt a natural repugnance to return to the land of captivity. His self-questionings and diffidence were in the end overcome by the mastering instinct of his soul; and to his religious imagination the instinct seemed to speak within him, like an inner voice, confirming his purpose. Such experiences befall men of a certain cast and mould when an impulse, which they can hardly justify when they weigh it in the scales of the understanding, affects them so strongly that it seems the objective compulsion or admonition of some external intelligence.

§3. *At Auxerre*

It is probable that when he was finally convinced of the destination of his life, and knew that he must seek the woods of Fochlad, Patrick did not tarry long in Britain, but returned to Gaul in order to prepare himself for carrying out his task. It was necessary not only to train himself, but to win support and countenance for his enterprise from influential authorities in the Church. Even if Patrick had been already in clerical orders, it would have been the mere adventure of a wild fanatic, and would have excited general disapprobation, to set sail in the first ship that left the mouth of the Severn for the Irish coast, and, trusting simply in his own zeal and the divine protection, set out to convert the heathen of Connaught. Such were not the conditions of the task which he aspired to perform. He knew that, if he was to succeed, he must come with support and resources and fellow-workers, accredited and in touch with the Christian communities which already existed in Ireland. He needed not only theological study and the counsels of men of leading and light, but material support and official recognition.

At this time the church of Autissiodorum seems to have already won a high position in northern Gaul through the virtues of its bishop, Amator. It was soon to win a higher fame still through the greater talents of Amator's successor. The town of Autissiodorum, situated on the river Yonne, is no exception to the general rule that the towns of Gaul have preserved the old Gallic names, whether place-names or tribe-names, throughout Roman and German domination alike; and Auxerre, like most towns in Gaul, unlike most towns in Britain, has had a continuous life through all changes since the days when it was Patrick's home in the reign of Honorius and Valentinian. For it was Auxerre that Patrick chose as the place of his study; perhaps he was introduced to Amator by British ecclesiastics. It may be that there was some special link or intimacy between the church of Auxerre and one of the British sees. But it is not unlikely that there was a further motive in determining Patrick's choice. Perhaps some particular interest had been exhibited at Auxerre in the Christian communities of Ireland. There is, in fact, evidence which points to the conclusion that Auxerre was a resort of Irish Christians for theological study. Patrick was ordained deacon by Bishop Amator before long, and it would seem that two other young men, who were afterwards to help the spread of Christianity in Ireland, were ordained at the same time. One of them was a native of south Ireland; his Irish name was Fith, but he took the name of Iserninus. The nationality of his companion, Auxilius, which the Irish made into Ausaille, is unknown.

Fourteen years passed, at the smallest computation, from the ordination of Patrick till the day came for setting forth to his chosen task. This long delay can hardly be accounted for by the necessities of an ecclesiastical training. There must have been other impediments and difficulties. He intimates himself that he was not encouraged. Those to whom he looked up for counsel considered his project rash and himself unqualified for such a work. His *rusticitas,* or want of liberal education, was urged against him; and perhaps a failure to win support is a sufficient explanation of the delay.

At all events Patrick, one would suppose, had a discreet, if not a sympathetic, guide in the head of the church of Auxerre. Amator had been succeeded by one who was to bear a more illustrious name in the ecclesiastical annals of Gaul. Germanus is a case, common in Gaul and elsewhere at this period, of a distinguished layman who held office in the State exchanging secular for ecclesiastical office. In the year 429 it devolved upon him to visit Britain, and this enterprise must have had a particular interest for Patrick. The poison of the serpent Pelagius, as his opponents named him, had been spreading, in a diluted form, in the island; some of the writings of its British advocates are still extant. The orthodox pillars of the British Church were alarmed, and they sent pressing messages across the sea to invite their Gallic brethren to send able champions over to overcome the heresy. It was probably to Auxerre and Troyes, in the first instance, that they made their appeal, and it is recorded that at a synod held at Troyes it was decided that Germanus should proceed to Britain along with Lupus, Bishop of Troyes, who had been formerly a monk of Lérins. Whatever may be the truth about this alleged Gallic synod, Germanus went with higher authority and prestige; for he went under the direct sanction of Celestine, the Bishop of Rome. We learn that this sanction was gained by the influence of the deacon Palladius, who may possibly have been a deacon of Germanus. The authoritative mission from Gaul seems to have crushed the heretics, and their doctrine was compelled to hide its head in Britain for a few years to come.

Celestine was approached soon afterwards on a subject which touched Patrick more closely than the suppression of heresy in Britain. His attention was drawn to the position of the Christian communities in Ireland. The man who interested himself in this matter was the same deacon, Palladius, who had interested himself in the extirpation of British Pelagianism. It is remarkable that this first appearance of Irish Christianity in ecclesiastical history should be associated, both chronologically and in the person of Palladius, with the Pelagian question. Now we may be sure that some overture or message had come from the Christian bodies in Ireland, whether to Britain, or Gaul, or to Rome itself; for the Bishop of Rome would hardly have sent them a bishop unless they had intimated that they wanted one.[7] It is, then, not impossible, though it is not proven, that the motive of the Irish Christians in taking such a step at this moment may have been the same Pelagian difficulty which had caused the appeal from Britain.[8] The question, which must have occurred sooner or later, of organising the small Christian societies of Ireland may possibly have been brought to a head by the Pelagian debate. And if the Pelagian heresy had gained any ground in Ireland, nothing would have been more natural than that the fact should have come before the notice of Germanus while he was dealing with the same question in Britain.

This conjecture, which is suggested unconstrainedly by the general situation, may supply us with the key for reading between the lines of a passage in Patrick's autobiographical sketch. He complains of the treachery of a most intimate friend, whom he does not name, but who seems, from the circumstances, to have been an ecclesiastic, whether of Britain or Gaul. To this friend he had communicated his inmost thoughts,—*credidi etiam animam,*—and had evidently received sympathy from him in regard to his cherished plan of working in Ireland. His friend had told him emphatically that he must be made a bishop. And afterwards, when the question of choosing a bishop for Ireland practically arose, his friend was active in urging his claims. Now it was in Britain that the matter was discussed when Patrick's friend, though Patrick himself was not there, showed such loyal zeal in his behalf. Here, then, we have an incident which exactly fits into the situation when Germanus was fighting against heresy in Britain in A.D. 429. If this heresy existed in Ireland, it was an element in the problem with which Germanus had to deal, even with regard to British interests solely; for, if the false doctrine were permitted to spread unchecked in the Irish communities, it might constitute a serious danger to the neighbouring church in Britain. If, as was most likely to occur, orthodox members of the Irish communities sent representatives to Germanus while he was in Britain and asked for some intervention, the question of sending a bishop to guide the Irish Christians in the right path and organise their society became at once practical and urgent. This then, it seems reasonable to suggest, may have been the occasion on which Patrick's friend designated him as the suitable man for the post.

The opportunity for which Patrick had been waiting long seemed to have come at last. Probably a certain interest in

Irish Christianity had been already felt in Gaul, and especially at Auxerre; but it was now brought under the notice of the head of Christendom. There seemed a prospect now for Patrick to undertake the work on which he had set his heart under high sanction and with sufficient support. But Celestine's choice fell on another. The deacon Palladius, who had been active in these affairs, was prepared to go to Ireland, and Celestine consecrated him bishop for the purpose (A.D. 431). The choice, if it was Celestine's own, was perfectly natural. We must remember that the first and chief consideration of Celestine was the welfare and orthodoxy of Irish believers, not the conversion of Irish unbelievers. He was called upon to meet the need of the Christian communities; the further spreading of the faith among the heathen was an ulterior consideration. The qualification, therefore, which he sought in the new bishop may not have been burning zeal for preaching to pagans, but rather experience and capacity for dealing with the Pelagian heresy. Palladius had taken a prominent part in coping with this heresy in Britain, and it is a probable conjecture that he had accompanied Germanus thither. Possibly representatives of the Irish Christians may have intimated that they wished for his appointment.

§4. *Palladius in Ireland* (A.D. 431–2)

The brief chronicle of the visit of Palladius to Ireland is that he came and went within a year. It is generally assumed that he had not the strength or tact to deal with the situation; that he departed in despair; that his mission was a failure. But our evidence hardly warrants this conclusion. We are told that he proceeded from Ireland to the land of the Picts in north Britain, and died there. But we cannot be sure that he did not intend to return. It is with north Leinster[9] and the hills of Wicklow that tradition associates the brief episode of Palladius. But we may be tempted to suspect that the expedition of Palladius to the country of the Picts was not an abandonment of Ireland, but was, on the contrary, part of his work in Ireland, and that it was not the Picts of north Britain, but some Christian communities existing among the Picts of Dalaradia in north Ireland, who were the object of his concern. The most probable conclusion seems that the episcopate of Palladius in Ireland was cut short, not by a voluntary desertion of his post, but by death.

We should like to know where were the dwelling-places of the Christians to whom Palladius was sent. Between the port where Wicklow of the Vikings now is, the port where Palladius landed, and the lonely glen of the two lakes by whose shores a cluster of churches was afterwards to spring up, stretched the lands of the children of Garrchu, and tradition said that the chief of this tribe regarded Palladius with disfavour. But his short sojourn is also associated with the foundation of three churches. It is possible that we may seek the site of a little house for praying, built by him or his disciples, on a high wooded hill that rises sheer enough on the left bank of the river Avoca, close to a long slanting hollow, down which, over grass or bushes, the eye catches the glimmer of the stream winding in the vale below, and rises beyond to the higher hills which bound the horizon. Here may have been the "House of the Romans," Tech na Róman, and Tigroney, the shape in which this name is concealed, may be a memorial

of the first missioner of Rome. But farther west, beyond the
hills, we can determine with less uncertainty another place
which tradition associated with the activity of Palladius, in
the neighbourhood of one of the royal seats of the lords of
Leinster. From the high rath of Dunlavin those kings had a
wide survey of their realm. Standing there, one can see westward to Mount Bladma, and northward, across the Plain
of Liffey, into the kingdom of Meath. More than a league
eastward from this fortress Palladius is said to have founded
a church which was known as the "domnach" or "Lord's
house" of the High-field, *Domnach Airte,* in a hilly region
which is strewn with the remnants of ancient generations.
The original church of this place has long since vanished,
and its precise site cannot be guessed with certainty, but it
gave a permanent name to the place. At Donard we feel with
some assurance that we are at one of the earliest homes of
the Christian faith in Ireland, not the earliest that existed,
but the earliest to which we can give a name.

There was a third church, seemingly the most important
of those which Palladius is said to have founded, Cell Fine,
"the Church of the Tribes," in which his tablets and certain
books and relics which he had brought from Rome were
preserved. Here, and perhaps here only, in the place, unknown to us, where his relics lay, was preserved the memory
of Palladius, a mere name. Whatever his qualities may have
been, he was too short a time in Ireland to have produced
a permanent impression. The historical significance of his
appearance there does not lie in any slight ecclesiastical or
theological successes he may have accomplished. It is significant because it was the first manifestation in Ireland of

the authority of Rome. The secular arm of Rome, in days when Rome was mightier—the arm of Agricola, the arm of Theodosius—had never reached the Scottic coast; it was not till after the mother of the Empire had been besieged and despoiled by barbarian invaders that her new spiritual dominion began to reach out to those remote shores which her worldly power had never sought to gain. The coming of Palladius was the first link in the chain which bound Ireland—for some centuries loosely—to the spiritual centre of western Europe.

But when, seeking vainly for traces of this first comer in the vales of the children of Garrchu or on the holy hill of Donard, we see the memorials in earth and stone of days before Palladius, we are reminded that, if his coming is significant, it is a fact more important still that no secular messengers of Rome had come before him. The superstitious and primitive customs of the island were protected and secured, pure and uncontaminated, by the barrier of sundering seas. If one of the early Roman Emperors had annexed Ireland to their British provinces, ideas of city life and civil government and administration would have been introduced which might have proved a more powerful solvent than Christianity of Celtic and Iberian barbarism. A Roman colonia, a number of Roman towns with municipal organisation, might, in a couple of hundred years, have produced a greater change in civilisation than all the little clerical communities which sprang up in the three or four centuries after the coming of Palladius. It would have been the task of the Roman government to put an end to the incessant petty wars between the kingdoms and tribes, *pacisque imponere morem.*

But the absence of such civilising influence protected and preserved the native traditions, and the curiosity of those who study the development of the human mind may be glad that Ireland lay safe and undisturbed at the end of the world, and that Palladius, nearly a hundred years after the death of Constantine, was the first emissary from Rome.

§5. *Consecration of Patrick* (A.D. 432)

The appointment of Palladius as bishop for the Scots had naturally affected the plans of Patrick. There was no longer any motive for delay in setting about the accomplishment of his project. There was no reason why, with the support of Auxerre and Bishop Germanus, he should not set forth, along with whatever coadjutors he could muster, and, under the auspices of the new bishop, begin the conversion of the heathen. All was arranged for his enterprise in the following year (A.D. 432), and the tradition is that he had already set out from Auxerre, accompanied by Segitius, an elderly presbyter, when the news reached Gaul that Palladius was dead. The announcement was brought by some of the companions of Palladius, and Patrick's plans were once more interrupted. But only for a moment. The circumstances seem to imply that there was a distinct understanding that he was to be the successor of Palladius, and Germanus consecrated him bishop immediately. And so it came about that, in the end, he started for the field of his work invested with the authority and office which would render his labours most effective.

Considerable preparations had, doubtless, been necessary. To carry out the ambitious scheme of converting heathen lands, there was needed not only a company of fellow-workers, but a cargo of "spiritual treasures" and ecclesiastical gear for the equipment of the new communities which were to be founded.[10] Money and treasure were indispensable, and however simple Patrick's faith may have been in the intrinsic potency of the gospel which he was inspired to preach, he was a man of thoroughly practical mind, and he knew that silver and gold and worldly wealth would be needed in dealing with pagan princes, and in the effective establishment of clerical communities.

The foregoing account of Patrick's setting forth for the field of his labours is based on a critical examination of the oldest sources. In later times men wished to believe that he, too, like Palladius, was consecrated by Celestine.[11] Such a consecration seemed both to add a halo of dignity to the national saint and to link his church more closely to the apostolic seat. We have no means of knowing whether Patrick set out before or after the death of Celestine,[12] but in any case the pious story is inconsistent with the oldest testimonies. Nor, even if there were room for doubt, would the question involve any point of theoretical or practical importance. By virtue of what had already happened, Ireland was, in principle, as closely linked to Rome as any western church. The circumstances of the consecration and mission of Palladius were significant; but whether his successor was ordained at Rome or at Auxerre, whether he was personally known to the Roman pontiff or not, was a matter of little moment. It will not be amiss, however, to dwell more fully on the situation.

The position of the Roman see at this period in the Western Church is often wrongly represented, or vaguely understood. At the end of the fourth century the bishops of Rome, beyond their acknowledged primacy in Christendom, possessed at least two important rights which secured them a large influence in the ecclesiastical affairs of the western provinces of the Empire.[13] The Roman see was recognised by imperial decrees of Valentinian I. and Gratian as a court to which clergy might appeal from the decisions of provincial councils in any part of the western portion of the Empire. Of not less practical importance was another distinctive prerogative, which, though not recognised by any formal enactment, was admitted and acted upon by the churches of the west. The Roman Church was regarded as the model church, and when doubtful points of discipline arose, the bishops of the Gallic or other provinces used to consult the Bishop of Rome for guidance, not as to a particular case, but as to a general principle. The answers of the Roman bishops to such questions are what are called *decretals*. No decretals are preserved older than those of Damasus,[14] and perhaps it was in his pontificate that the practice of such applications for advice became general. The motive of the custom is evident. It was to preserve uniformity of discipline throughout the Church and prevent the upgrowth of divergent practices. But those who consulted the Roman pontiff were not in any way bound to accept his ruling. The decretal was an answer to a question; it was not a command. Those who accepted it were merely imitating the Roman see; they were not obeying it.

The appellate jurisdiction, and the decretals which were gradually to be converted from letters of advice into letters of command, were the chief foundations on which the spiritual empire of Rome grew up. But in the latter part of the fourth century its nascent authority was confronted by a serious danger in the shape of a rival. When Milan instead of Rome became the imperial residence in Italy, the see of Milan assumed immediately a new importance and prestige. Its bishop soon came to be regarded as an authority to which appeals might be addressed, as well as to the Bishop of Rome. This new dignity was justified by the personality of Ambrose, who then occupied the see, but it was due to the presence of the Augustus. If his presence had been lasting, it is possible that Mediolanum would have become in regard to Rome what Constantinople became, because it was the Imperial city, in regard to Alexandria and Antioch. But the danger passed away when the Emperor Honorius migrated to Ravenna, though the consequences of the transient rivalry of Milan with Rome can be traced for a few years longer.

For the further development of the spiritual authority of Rome two things were necessary—tact and imperial support. Bishop Zosimus possessed neither, and his brief pontificate did as much as could be done within two short years to injure the prestige of the apostolic seat. He was smitten on one cheek by the synods of Africa, he was smitten on the other by the Gallic bishops at the Council of Turin.[15] He intervened in the Pelagian controversy, and was obliged to eat his own words. But his inglorious pontificate remains a landmark,[16] because he was the first to make a strenuous attempt to exercise sovran rights which the western churches had never admitted or been asked to admit—rights which a more competent pontiff afterwards secured. The indiscretions of Zosimus were atoned for by more moderate successors, but the most consummate tact and adroitness would never have won the powers of intervention which he had claimed and the Gallic bishops had repudiated, if Pope Leo had not gained *the* ear of the Emperor. In A.D. 445, one of the greatest dates in the history of the growth of the papal power, the Emperor Valentinian III. conferred on the Bishop of Rome sovran authority in the western provinces which were still under imperial sway.[17]

But in the meantime, though southern Gaul might resist Zosimus and disregard Celestine when they attempted to assert a right of control, though Celestine might discern in the power of the see of Arles and in the tendencies of the monks of Lérins forces adverse to Roman influence, no Gallic bishop would have thought of questioning the appellate jurisdiction or the moral authority of the Roman see, as exercised before the days of Zosimus. Germanus of Auxerre might sympathise with Hilary of Arles in his struggle with Pope Leo, but in dealing with heresy in Britain he had acted cordially with Pope Celestine. No one could ascribe more importance than Vincentius of Lérins to the decisions of the "apostolic seat."[18] It would be a grave mistake to infer from the disputes which cluster round Arles that the bishops of Gaul had ceased in any way to acknowledge the older claims of Rome or to reverence it as the head of Christendom.

When a new ecclesiastical province was to be added to western Christendom, it was to Rome, naturally, that an appeal would be made. It was to the Bishop of Rome, as representing the unity of the Church, that the Christians of Ireland, desiring to be an organised portion of that unity, would naturally look to speed them on their way. His recognition of Ireland as a province of the spiritual federation of which he was the acknowledged head, would be the most direct and effective means of securing for it an established place among the western churches. If, then, they asked Celestine either to choose a bishop for them, or to confirm their own choice and consecrate a bishop of their choosing, they adopted exactly the course which we might expect. But once this step was taken, once the Roman bishop had given his countenance and sanction, it was a matter of indifference who consecrated his successor. There was significance in the consecration at Rome of the first bishop of the new province; there would have been no particular significance in such a consecration in the case of the second any more than in the case of the third. It was an accident that Patrick was consecrated in Gaul. If Palladius had not been cut off, and if Patrick had proceeded, as he intended, to Ireland in the capacity of a simple deacon, he might afterwards have been called to succeed Palladius by the choice of the Irish Christians and received episcopal ordination wherever it was most convenient. The essential point is that by the sending of Palladius, Ireland had become one of the western churches, and therefore, like its fellows, looked to the see of Rome as the highest authority in Christendom. Unless, at the very moment of incorporation, they were to repudiate the unity of the Church, the Christians of Ireland could not look with other eyes than the Christians of Gaul at the appellate jurisdiction of the Roman bishop, and the moral weight of his decretals.

IV

POLITICAL AND SOCIAL CONDITION
OF IRELAND

NOWHERE more conspicuously than in Ireland have secular institutions determined the manner in which the Christian religion spread and increased. The introduction of that religion effected no social revolution; it introduced new ideas and a new profession, but society steadily remained in the primitive stage of tribal organisation for more than a thousand years after the island had become part of Christendom.[1]

Ireland was divided into a large number of small districts, each of which was owned by a tribe,[2] the aggregate of a number of clans or families which believed that they were descended from a common ancestor. At the head of the tribe was a "king," who was elected from a certain family. Below the king were four social grades within the tribe. There were the nobles,[3] who were distinguished by the possession of land. These were the only members of the tribe, besides the king, who had land of their own. After them came those who had wealth in cattle and other movable property,[4] but were only tenants of the land on which they lived. Below these were freemen, who had no property either in soil or in cattle, but farmed lands for which they paid rent. The lowest grade consisted of herds and labourers of various kinds, who were not freemen, but were regarded as members of the tribe and entitled to its protection. There was also another class of slaves who did not belong to the tribe, consisting of strangers—such as fugitives, bought slaves, and captives. Patrick belonged to this class, *fudirs* as they were called, in the days of his bondage.

Originally all the land must have belonged to the tribe. But at the time with which we are concerned, part of the arable land was the private property of the king and the nobles. There were, however, certain restrictions on this proprietorship which show that, theoretically, all the land was still considered as in a certain sense tribal. The chief of these was that the proprietor could not alienate his land without the consent of the tribe.

The limits of these small tribal kingdoms can be still approximately traced, for they are represented, for the most part, by the baronies of the modern map, and the names of the baronies in many cases preserve the names of the tribes. The inspection of a map on which the baronies are marked will convey a general idea of the number and size of the small kingdoms which formed the political units of the island. These kingdoms varied greatly in size; the tribes varied in numbers and importance. But each kingdom, whether large or small, managed its own affairs. The self-government of the tribes, and the complicated organisation of the clans and families within them, were the most important and fundamental social facts. But the tribal units were grouped together loosely in a political organisation of an elaborate kind, consisting in degrees of overlordship.

Thus the king of Cashel was king over all the kingdoms of Munster; the under-kings owed him tribute and service in war, and he had certain obligations to them.[5] The king of Connaught and the king of Laigin held the same position in regard to the kings of those provinces, and the King of Tara exercised similar overlordship over the kings of Meath. But the king of Tara was also overlord of all the kings of Ireland, and his superior position was designated by the title "Árd-rí," High King.

The kings of Cashel, Connaught, and Laigin are usually described as provincial kings. For the island was regarded as consisting of five provinces or "fifths." Connaught, Mumen, and "Ultonia" corresponded, with some minor differences, to Connaught, Munster, and Ulster of the modern map; while Leinster represents the two remaining fifths, Laigin in the south and Meath in the north. But it does not appear that in historical times there was any king who held the same position in the province of Ulster which the king of Cashel held in Munster. The northern province consisted of three large kingdoms, which seem to have been wholly independent, Aileach, Oriel, and Ulaid.[6] The kings of these territories were all alike overlords of under-kings; they were all alike subject to the High King; but they were as independent of one another as they were of the king of Connaught. The king of Ulaid was not under the king of Aileach, as the king of Thomond or the king of Ossory was under the king of Cashel.[7]

Ireland then was organised, theoretically, in an ascending scale of kings and over-kings. There was the High King at the head of all. Below him were six over-kings, the king of

Cashel, the king of Connaught, the king of Laigin, the king of Aileach, the king of Ulaid, and the king of Oriel. Below these were the tribal kings, but in some cases there were intermediate grades, kings who were overlords of several small territories. For example, several of the small kingdoms in north Munster formed an intermediate group, the kingdom of Thomond. It is clear that this system must have grown up by degrees through conquest, and one remarkable practice illustrates its origin. It was the habit of the over-kings to take hostages from the under-kings, as a surety for the fulfilment of their obligations. This was such an important feature of the political system that a house for the custody of hostages was an almost indispensable addition to a royal palace. The "mound of the hostages" is still shown at Tara.[8]

But though the general theory of the system is clear, it would be difficult to say how far it was a reality at any particular period, or how far the elaborate scheme of obligations and counter-obligations, binding on the kings of all ranks, was intended to be enforced. The ceaseless warfare which marks the annals of Ireland suggests that these bonds were a cause of trouble rather than a source of union.

Of the political relations existing in Ireland in the fifth century we know practically nothing. The most important fact seems to be that the descendants of King Eochaid,[9] and particularly the family of his son Niall, both of whom had been High Kings, were winning a decided preponderance in the northern half of the island. When Patrick came to Ireland, a son of Niall was on the throne of Tara; his cousin was king of Connaught; one of his sons gave an abiding name to a large territory in north Ulster;[10] other sons were kings of

lesser kingdoms in Meath. Family connexions of this kind
were no permanent, or even immediate, guarantee of union;
but it is probable that at this time, through the predominance
of his near kindred, a prudent High King, such as Loigaire,
son of Niall, seems to have been, may have been able to
exert more effectual and far-reaching influence than many
of his forerunners and successors. We shall have occasion to
observe that his reign seems to have been a relatively peaceful
period, if such an epithet can be applied to any epoch of Irish
history. Whatever may have been the measure of the High
King's authority, it was unquestionably desirable for the new
bishop, in pursuing his designs, to secure his favour or neu-
trality. But the political situation and the mutual relations of
the higher potentates had, we may fairly surmise, no decisive
or serious effect on the prospects of the religion which was
now about to become firmly established in the land. Those
prospects depended mainly, if not entirely, upon gaining the
tribal kings and the heads of families. The king of Ulidia,
or the King of Ireland himself, might suffer or encourage
the strange worship in his own immediate territory, might
himself embrace the faith, but beyond that he could only rec-
ommend it; and though his example might indeed do much,
he could not force any under-king and his tribe to tolerate
the presence of a Christian community in their borders.

It was not political relations but the tribal system and
economic conditions that claimed the study of a bishop who
came not merely to make individual converts, but to build
up a sacerdotal society. A church and a priesthood must have
means of support, and in a country where wealth consisted in
land and cattle it was plain that, if the church was to become

a stable and powerful institution, its priests and ministers must have lands secured for their use. But land could be obtained only through the goodwill of those who possessed it, and therefore it was impossible to plant a church in any territory until some noble who owned a private estate had been persuaded to accept the Christian baptism and to make a grant of land for ecclesiastical use, with his tribe's consent. The conversion of the landless classes, slaves, or farmers, or even the lords of herds, could not lead to the foundation of churches and the maintenance of sacerdotal institutions. The success of Patrick's enterprise depended on the kings of the tribes and the chiefs of the clans.

There was another reason also why Christianity could not hope to make considerable progress until the heads of society had been converted. Strong tribal sentiment, expressed in the devotion of the tribesmen to the king of the tribe, of the clansmen to the chief of the clan, was the most powerful social bond; and while, if a chief accepted the new faith, his clan would generally follow his example, it was not likely that if he rejected it many of his followers would dissociate themselves from his action. Thus on every account the process of establishing the Christian worship and priesthood in Ireland must begin from above and not from below.

We know little of the religious beliefs and cults in Ireland which the Christian faith aspired to displace. If there was any one divinity who was revered and worshipped throughout the land it was probably the sun. There seem to have been no temples, but there were altars in the open air, and idols were worshipped, especially in the form of pillar-stones. Various gods and goddesses play a part in the tales of Irish mythology, but it is not known whether any of these beings was honoured by a cult. There was no priesthood, and it seems certain that there was no organised religion which could be described as national.

Heathenism of such a kind could oppose no formidable resistance to the weapons of such a force as the organised religion which had swept the Roman Empire. Heathenism is naturally tolerant; and, when there is no powerful sacerdotal order jealous of its privileges and monopoly, a new superstition is readily entertained. It must be admitted as probable that the morality which the Christian faith enjoins, and the hopes which it offers, would hardly have appealed to heathen peoples or taken possession of their minds if it had not engaged their imaginations by mysteries and rites. It was, above all, these mysterious rites—baptism, without which the body and soul were condemned to everlasting torment, and the mystical ceremony which is known as the Eucharist—that stamped the religion as genuine in the eyes of barbarians. And it is to be observed that Christianity, while it demanded that its converts should abandon heathen observances and heathen cults, did not require them to surrender their belief in the existence of the beings whom they were forbidden to worship. They were only required to regard those beings in a new light, as maleficent demons. For the Christians themselves, even the highest authorities in the Church, were as superstitious as the heathen. The belief in the *sidhe,* or fairies, which was universal in Ireland, was not affected by Christianity, and survives at the present day. Thus the spreading of the new religion was facilitated by the circumstance that it made no attempt to root out the heathen superstitions as intellectual absurdities, but only aimed at transcending and transforming them, so that fear of deities should be turned into hatred of demons.

The chief pretenders to the possession of wizardry and powers of divination in Ireland were the Druids,[11] who correspond, but not in all respects, to the Druids of Gaul. They joined to their supernatural lore innocent secular learning, skill in poetry, and knowledge of the laws and history of their country. They gave the kings advice and educated their children. The high value which was attached to their counsels rested naturally on their prophetic powers. They practised divination in various forms, with inscribed rods of yew, for instance, or by means of magic wheels.[12] They could raise the winds, cover the plains with darkness, create envelopes of vapour,[13] which rendered those who moved therein invisible. Though learned in things divine, they did not form a sacerdotal class; and in their religious functions they might be compared rather to augurs than to priests. It was their habit to shave their heads in front from ear to ear and to wear white garments. It was inevitable that these men should be unfriendly to the introduction of new beliefs which threatened their own position, since it condemned the practice of divination and those kindred arts on which their eminent power was based. But their opposition could not be effective, because they had no organisation.

The fact, then, that the Christian Church, by its recognition of demons as an actual power with which it had to cope, stood in this respect on the same intellectual plane as the heathen, was an advantage in the task of diffusing the religion. The belief in demons as a foe with which the Church had

to deal was expressed officially in the institution of a clerical
order called exorcists, whose duty it was, by means of formulae, to exorcise devils at baptism.[14] Patrick had exorcists
in his train, and it was not unimportant that the Christian,
going forth to persuade the heathen, had such equipments
of superstition. He was able to meet the heathen sorcerer on
common ground because he believed in the sorceries which
he condemned.[15] He was as fully convinced as the pagan that
the powers of magicians were real, but he knew that those
powers were strictly limited, whereas the power of his own
God was limitless. Patrick could never have said to an Irish
wizard, as children of enlightenment would now say, "Your
magic is imposture; your spells cannot really raise spirits or
control the forces of nature; you cannot foretell what is to
come." He would have said, "Yes, you can do such miracles by the aid of evil powers, but those powers are subject
to a good power whose religion I preach, and are impotent
except through his permission." This point of mental agreement between the Christian priest and the heathen whom he
regarded as benighted, their common belief in the efficacy
of sorcery, though they put different interpretations on its
conditions,[16] was probably not an insignificant aid in the
propagation of the Christian religion. It may be said, more
generally, that if Christianity had offered to men only its
new theological doctrine with the hope of immortal life and
its new ethical ideals, if it had come simple and unadorned,
without an armoury of mysteries, miracles, and rites, if it
had risen to the height of rejecting magic not because it was
wicked but because it was absurd, it could never have won
half the world.

It was natural that the spread of new religious ideas should excite the misgivings of the Druids, but so long as the new doctrine was professed only here and there in isolated households, they could hardly gauge its force or estimate the danger. It is not unlikely that shortly before the coming of Palladius they awoke to the fact that a faith, opposed to their own interests, was gaining ground, for, at the same time, the Christian communities were discovering that they deserved and required a bishop and an ecclesiastical organisation. The apprehension of the Druids may be reflected in a prophecy attributed to the wizards of the High King. They foretold that a foreign doctrine would seduce the people, overthrow kings, and subvert the old order of things, and they designated the preacher of the doctrine in these oracular words: "Adze-head will come with a crook-head staff; in his house, with hole-head robe, he will chant impiety from his table; from the front (eastern) part of his house all his household will respond, So be it, so be it." It would not be legitimate to build any theory on an alleged prophecy, when we cannot control its date. But we may admit, without hesitation, that this ancient verse, which was assuredly composed by a pagan, contains nothing inconsistent with the tradition that it was current before the coming of Patrick. There is nothing to stamp it as an oracle *post eventum*. The knowledge which it shows of Christian usages was accessible to the Druids, inasmuch as Christianity was already known, had already won converts, in Ireland. And if, as we have seen reason to believe, the Christians of Ireland negotiated for the appointment of a bishop a year or two before the sending of Palladius, there would be no difficulty in supposing that the Druids at this juncture, aware that a leader was expected, expressed their apprehensions in this form. But whatever be the truth about the oracle, whether it circulated in the mouths of men before the appearance of Palladius and Patrick, or was first declared at a later period, it possesses historical significance as reflecting the agitation of heathenism, roused at length to alarm at the growth of the foreign worship.

V

IN THE ISLAND-PLAIN, IN DALARADIA

THE spot where the river Vartry, once the Dee, reaches the coast, just north of the long ness which runs out into the sea at Wicklow, has a historical interest because this little river mouth, now of no account, was a chief port of the island in ancient times for mariners from south Britain and Gaul, a place where strangers and traders landed, and where the natives could perhaps most often have sight of outlandish ships and foreign faces. It was the port where Patrick would most naturally land coming from south Britain; but in any case he could hardly do otherwise than first seek the region where Palladius had briefly laboured. This would naturally be the starting-point, the place for studying the situation, forming plans, perhaps opening negotiations. But there is no record of this first indispensable stage in the new bishop's work, and our ignorance of his relations to these communities in southern Ireland is one of the most unhappy gaps in our meagre knowledge of his life. He has no sooner landed in the kingdom of Leinster than tradition transports him to the kingdom of Ulidia.

We must see where this tradition—this Ulidian tradition—would lead, though we cannot allow it to guide us blindly. There are two connected narratives professing to describe important passages of Patrick's work in Ireland.

One of these[1] contains some genuine, unvarnished records as to Christian communities which he founded. The other[2] is compact of stories which it is difficult to utilise for historical purposes, though it be admitted that they have elements of historical value. The most striking parts of it are pure legend, but they are framed in a setting which might include some literal facts. And the historical background is there, though we have to allow for some distortion by anti-pagan motives. But the difficulty which meets the critic here is due to the circumstance that he has no sufficient records of a genuine historical kind to guide him in dealing with this mixed material. Most of those who have undertaken to deal with it have adopted the crude and vain method of retaining as historical what is not miraculous. There is much which we can securely reject at once, but there are other things which, while we are not at liberty to accept them, we must regard as possibly resting on some authentic basis. We have not the data for a definite solution. It has seemed best, then, to reproduce the story, to criticise it, and point out what may be its implications.

If we stand on the steep headland which towers above the sea halfway between the Danish towns of Wicklow and Dublin, the eye reaches from the long low hill prominence under which the southern town is built, northward to the island of Lambay. A little beyond, hidden from the view and close to the coast, are some small islets which in ancient days were known as the isles of the Children of Cor. If we could see these minute points of land, we should be able to take in, with a sweep of the eye, the first stage of St Patrick's traditional journey when he steered his boat northward from the mouth of the Dee to bear his message to the woods and glens of Ulidia. The story tells that he landed on one of these islets, which has ever since been known as Inis Patrick. The name attests an association with the apostle. It might be said that, if he travelled to Ulidia by sea, as he may well have done, it was a natural precaution, in days when travellers might be suspected as outlaws or robbers, to land for a night's halt on a desert island rather than on the coast, where churlish inhabitants might give a stranger no pleasant welcome. From the island which bears his name he continued his course along the coast of Meath, past the mouth of the Boyne, and along the shores of Conaille Muirthemni, which formed the southern part of the Ulidian kingdom. This was the country where in old days Setanta,[3] the lord of the march, is said to have kept watch and ward over the gates of Ulster. But it was in more northern parts of the Pictish kingdom that Patrick's purpose lay, and he steered on past the inlet which was not yet the fiord of the Carlings, past the mountainous region of southern Dalaradia, till he came to a little land-locked bay, which in shape, though on a far smaller scale, and not flanked by mountains, resembles the Bay of Pagasae. But the sea-portal to Lake Strangford, as it is now called, is a much narrower strait[4] than the mouth of the Greek gulf. Patrick rowed into this water, and landed, he and those that were with him, on the southern shore of the bay at the mouth of the Slan stream, which till recent years was known by its old name.[5] They hid their boat, we are told, and went a short distance inward from the shore to find a place of rest. Had they rowed farther westward and followed, past salt marshes, the banks of the winding river Quoile, they would

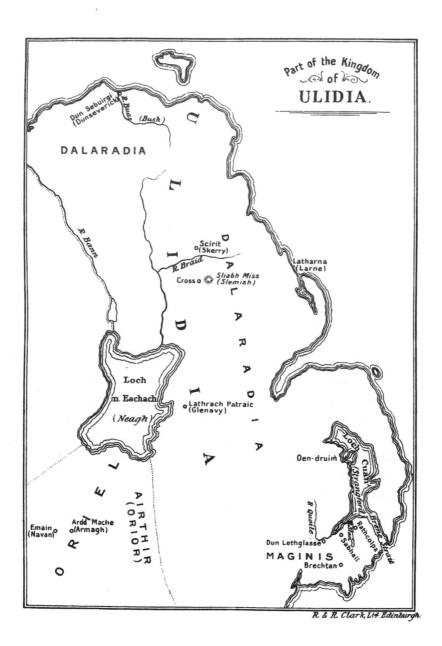

Part of the Kingdom
of
ULIDIA.

DALARADIA

U L I D I A

Dun Sebuirgi
(Dunseverick)

R. Buas (Bush)

R. Bann

Scirit
(Skerry)

R. Braid

D A L A R A D I A

Latharna
(Larne)

Cross o ☼ Sliabh Miss
(Slemish)

Loch

m. Eachach

(Neagh)

Lathrach Patraic
(Glenavy)

O R I E L

A I R T H I R
(ORIOR)

Emain
(Navan)

Ardd Mache
(Armagh)

Oen-druim

Loch
Cuan
(Strangford
Lough)

R. quaile

Dun Lethglasse

Rathcolpa
Sabhall

MAGINIS
Brechtan

R. & R. Clark, Ltd Edinburgh.

have soon come to a great fortress, Dún Lethglasse. But of the country and the country's folk the tale supposes that they knew nought. A swineherd espied the strangers from his hut, and, supposing them to be thieves and robbers, went forth and told his master. The region is embossed, as it were, with small hills, and one of the higher of these hills was the master's abode. Dichu was the name of this man of substance, and he was one of those "naturally good" men whom Patrick, though he was not a Pelagian, may have been prepared to find among pagan folk. At the tidings of his herd, Dichu was prepared to slay the strangers, but when he looked upon the face of Patrick he changed his mind and offered hospitality. Then Patrick preached to him and he believed, the first convert won by the apostle in the land of the Scots.

Before we ask the questions that naturally rise in the mind when we hear a tale like this, we must accompany the saint on a further stage in his progress. He tarried with Dichu only a few days, for he was impatient to carry out a purpose which he cherished of revisiting the scene of his thraldom and the home of his old master Miliucc in the extreme north of Dalaradia. He left his boat in the keeping of Dichu and journeyed by land through the country of the Picts till he saw once more the slopes of Mount Miss. Miliucc still lived, and Patrick wished to pay the master from whom he had fled the price of his freedom. It is not suggested that he deemed it necessary, even after so many years, thus to legalise his liberty and secure himself against the claim of a master to seize a fugitive slave. The suggestion seems rather to be that he hoped to convert Miliucc to the Christian doctrine, and that the best means of conciliation was to recognise his right. But the heathen chief, hearing that he was approaching with this intent, and seized with a strange alarm lest his former slave should by some irresistible spell constrain him to embrace a new religion against his will, resorted to an extreme device. Having gathered all his substance together into his wooden house, he set fire to the building, and perished with it. The flames of the unexpected pyre met Patrick's eyes as he stood on the south-western side of Mount Miss,[6] and his biographer pictures him standing for two or three hours dumb with surprise and grief. "I know not, God knows," he said, using a favourite phrase, "whether the posterity of this man shall not serve others for ever, and no king arise from his seed." Then he turned back and retraced his steps to the habitation of Dichu.

The funeral pyre of Mount Miss[7] sends our thoughts over sea and land to a more famous pyre at Sardis. The self-immolation of the obscure Dalaradian kingling belongs to the same cycle of lore as that of the great Lydian monarch whose name became a proverb for luxury and wealth. Croesus built a timber death-pile in the court of his palace to escape the shame of servitude to an earthly conqueror; Miliucc sought the flames to avoid the peril of thraldom under a ghostly master. But in both cases the idea of a king dying solemnly by fire is taken from some old religious usage and introduced by legendary fancy into an historical situation. And in this case fancy has wrought well and fitly. The desperate pyre of Miliucc is a pathetic symbol of the protest of a doomed religion.

The "island-plain"[8] of Dalaradia and the districts about Dún Lethglasse claimed to have been the part of Ireland in which Patrick began his work of preaching and baptizing heathen men. He abode there and his religion grew; and inhabitants of those places in later days, when his memory had been glorified, pleased themselves by the thought that he "chose out and loved" this plain. He established himself securely here with the help of his friend Dichu, who, though apparently not the lord of Dún Lethglasse, was clearly a chieftain of influence and authority in that region. Dichu granted Patrick a site for a Christian establishment on a hill not far from the fortress, and a wooden barn was said to have been turned into a place of Christian worship. The rustic association has been preserved in the name, which has remained ever since, *Sabhall* or *Saul*, a word said to be borrowed[9] from the Latin *stabulum*—cattle-stall or sheepfold.

We cannot suppose that the history of St Patrick's first plunge into his missionary work was so simple, or so fully left to the play of chance, as this naive tale represents. It belongs to a class of tales which are characteristic of history in its uncritical stage, tales which invert the perspective and magnify some subordinate incident to be the main motive and purpose of the actors, ignoring the true motive or depressing it to the level of an accident. Such tales, which abounded, for instance, in the records of Hellas, are often accepted as literally true if they hang together superficially, and if the particular incidents are natural or even possible. A deeper criticism displays their incredibility. The epic simplicity of Patrick's journey may be true to outward circumstances, but it is not possible to believe that he went out so purely at a venture, like one in a romance who fares forth, on a quest indeed and with a purpose, yet content to leave his course to be guided by fortune, without previous plan or calculation. The sole motive of Patrick's northern journey is represented here as the hope of persuading his old master to become a Christian, whereas its actual and important result, the missionary work in southern Ulidia, appears almost as an accidental consequence. The hard historic fact which underlies the story is the work of Patrick in Ulidia and the foundation of Saul; and the story is evidently the Ulidian legend of this beginning of a new epoch in Ulidian history. Recognising this, we are unable to trust the story even so far as to infer that Ulidia was the first scene of Patrick's missionary activity, as the Ulidians claimed. We can neither affirm this nor deny it; but we must observe that, according to another tradition, which has just as much authority, he began his work in the kingdom of Meath. We have already seen reason to reject the tradition that the place of Patrick's captivity was in north-eastern Ireland, and we may now see this record in a new light, as part of an attempt of the Ulidian Christians to appropriate, as it were, Patrick to themselves, to associate with their own land the bondage of his boyhood and to make it the stage of his earliest labours.

There is one point in the story which can be accepted. It can be shown that Dichu, the proprietor of Saul, was a real person. He was the son of Trechim, and his brother Rus was a man of influence who lived at Brechtan, which is still Bright, a few miles south of Saul. But was this region so completely unprepared for the reception of the new faith as the legend represents? Was the Christian idea a new revelation to the chieftains of Dalaradia, borne for the first time by Patrick to those shores? It seems more probable that there were some

Christian communities there already and that the land was ripe for conversion. It has been pointed out above that it was perhaps in this land of the Picts that Palladius died. If this were so—but we are treading on ground where certainty is unattainable—we might accept without much hesitation the Ulidian claim that, when Patrick left Leinster, his first destination was Ulidia. For it would be the first duty of the new bishop of the Christians in Ireland to visit and confirm the Christian communities which existed. The force of the argument depends on the fact that two different lines converge to a fixed point. The action of Palladius, the first bishop of Ireland, in leaving Leinster and sailing "to the land of the Picts," and the Ulidian tradition that Patrick also travelled directly from Leinster to the land of the Picts, may find a common solution in the hypothesis that the Christian faith had already taken root in Dalaradia.

Other churches in the neighbourhood of Saul claimed to have been planted by Patrick, one at Brechtan, the place of Dichu's brother, another at Rathcolpa, which is still Raholp. Brechtan was the church of his disciple, Bishop Loarn; and Tassach, his artificer, who made altars and other things which were needed for his religious rites and the furnishing forth of his oratories, was installed at Rathcolpa. These three places, associated intimately with the first growth of Christianity in the Ulidian kingdom, Saul, Brechtan, and Rathcolpa, are ranged, within a short distance, on the eastern side of the Dún, which, a place of some note in Ireland's secular history, was destined to win importance as a religious centre. But no church was founded there by St Patrick, though his name was afterwards to become permanently attached to it. The most interesting remains of past ages at Down-patrick are not ecclesiastical, but the "down" or dún itself, a great mound encircled by three broad ramparts on the banks of the Quoile, one of the most impressive of ancient Irish earth-works.

The most irreproachable contemporary evidence could hardly testify more clearly to the deep impression that St Patrick made upon the dwellers of the Island - plain than the fact that their mythopoeic instinct was stirred, at a very early stage, to explain one of the natural features of their country by the miraculous powers of their teacher. According to one story an uncivil and grasping neighbour seized two oxen of St Patrick, which were at pasture. The saint cursed him: "Mudebrod! thou hast done ill. Thy land shall never profit thee." And on the same day the sea rushed in and covered it, and the fruitful soil was changed into a salt marsh. The motive of such tales is to account for the origin of the salt marshes which mark the northern border of the island-plain on the shores of Lake Strangford,[10] and they show that the figure of St Patrick had inspired popular imagination in those regions at an early period.

VI

IN MEATH

§1. *King Loigaire's Policy*

IT has been already pointed out that the Roman termi-
nus did not mark the limit of Roman influence. That
influence extended beyond the bounds of the Empire. The
existence of the majestic Empire was a fact of which its free
neighbours had to take cognisance, and which impressed
itself on their minds as one of the great facts of the universe. They were forced into intercourse, whether hostile or
peaceful, with the Roman republic. We have seen that it
must have affected the folks of Ireland who were the neighbours of the British and Gallic provinces, though severed by
narrow seas. The soil of that island had indeed never been
trodden by Roman legions, but its ports were not sealed to
the outer world, and from the first century the outer world
practically meant the Roman world. The men of Ireland
in the fourth century must have conceived their island as
lying just outside the threshold of a complex of land and
sea, over which the power of Rome stretched to bounds almost inaccessible to their imagination. When the grasp of
Rome relaxed or her power grew weak in the neighbouring provinces of Britain, the Irish speedily became aware,
and, like the Germans, failed not to seize opportunities for

winning spoil and plunder; but, though they appear in
Roman records as wasters and enemies, this does not imply that they had no respect and veneration for Rome and
her civilisation. The compatibility of veneration with hostile
behaviour on the part of barbarians is shown by the attitude of the Germans in all their dealings with the Empire
which they dismembered. We may be sure that the Iberians
and Celts of Ireland, who were certainly not inferior in intelligence to the Germans or less open to new ideas, were
qualified to admire the majesty of the Roman name and to
feel curiosity about the immense empire which dominated
their horizon. Some of their own folk, as we saw, had found
new habitations in Roman territory,[1] and thus formed a special channel for Roman influence to trickle into the free
island.

The chief influence was the infiltration of the Christian
religion. The adoption of this religion by the Imperial government in the fourth century must have had, as we have
seen, a sensible effect in conferring prestige on Christianity
beyond the boundaries of the Empire. It became inevitable
that the favoured creed should henceforth be closely associated with the Empire in the idea of barbarians and regarded
as the Roman religion. Hence that religion acquired, on
political grounds, a higher claim on their attention.

We must realise the force of these general considerations
in order to understand the policy of the High King who sat
on the throne of Ireland throughout the whole period of
Patrick's work in the island. Loigaire had succeeded about
five years before Patrick's arrival (A.D. 428). He was son of
King Niall, who had been slain in Britain, perhaps in the very

year in which Patrick had been carried into captivity. Niall's immediate successor was his nephew, Dathi, who reigned for twenty-three years, and likewise found death beyond the sea. But Dathi, it would seem, went forth as a friend, not as a foe, of Rome. He led a host to help the Roman general Aetius to drive back the Franks from the frontiers of eastern Gaul, and he was struck by lightning. The expedition of Dathi has an interest not only from the Irish, but also from the Roman point of view. It illustrates the wide view of Aetius. It shows us how he looked to all quarters for mercenary help; if he relied on the Huns, whom he was hereafter to smite so hard, he also invited auxiliaries from Scottia. From the Irish side, it illustrates the fact that Ireland was within the Roman horizon.

The reign of Loigaire lasted thirty-six years, and it marks a new epoch in Irish history. The part which Loigaire himself played in bringing about this change has been underrated. His statesmanship has been obscured by tradition, but is revealed by interrogation of the scanty evidence.

The first difficulty is one which meets us at all stages of early Irish history. It is impossible to determine the compass of the power and authority of the High Kings in the under-kingdoms. It seems probable that Loigaire was able to exercise as much influence, at least in northern Ireland, as was permitted to any king by the political and social organisation of the country. We have seen that the efforts of his grandfather, Eochaid, and his father, Niall, had extended the power of the family throughout a great part of north Ireland. His cousin, Amolngaid, was king of Connaught. His brothers and half-brothers were petty kings.[2]

Whatever the authority of Loigaire was, he seems to have used it in the interests of peace. So far as we can judge from the evidence of the Annals, his reign was a period of peace. He was indeed the perpetual enemy of the king of Leinster, and on three occasions at least there was war between them. On the first, Loigaire was victorious; on the second, he was taken prisoner; on the third, he was slain. But apart from this fatal feud we do not hear of wars, and we do not hear that he ventured upon expeditions over sea or took advantage of the difficulties of Britain, engaged then in her struggle with the invaders who were to conquer her.

A pacific policy harmonises with the record—though a warlike policy would not contradict it—that in his reign and under his auspices a code of native laws was constructed. This code, entitled the *Senchus Mór,* still exists, changed and enlarged, and something will be said of it in another place. It seems probable that the idea of this national work was due to the example and influence of the Roman Empire. There is no direct evidence that this was so, but it is a remarkable co-incidence that the reign of the king to whom the Irish code is ascribed concurs with the reign of the Emperor Theo-dosius, whose lawyers gathered the imperial edicts into the code called by his name. It cannot be thought improbable that this coincidence is significant, and that the influence of Rome is responsible for the earlier code of the Scot no less than for the later codes of Goth, Burgundian, and Frank. The synchronism struck the native annalists, and they ex-pressed it in a clumsy way by placing the composition of the Irish law-book in the very year in which the Code of Theodosius was issued (A.D. 438). That may be taken as a naive unhistorical expression of a true discernment that the idea of the Code of Loigaire and his colleagues came directly or indirectly from the Empire.

The way in which the Roman world made its influence felt in Ireland should be compared with the ways in which it exerted influence over other adjacent countries. Let us take, for instance, Russia. Neither Russia nor Ireland ever passed for a moment under the rule of Caesar. Both states were neighbours of the Empire, and for the kings of Tara as for the princes of Kiev the Empire was the eminent fact in the political worlds with which they were acquainted. In both cases the intercourse of trade, varied by warfare, prepared the way for the ultimate reception of some of the ideas of the higher culture of Rome. But there was one essential difference, due to political geography. Ireland was of little consequence or account in the eyes of the Caesars of Old Rome, and it was only now and then, as in the days of Valentinian I., that they were called upon to give it a thought; whereas for the Caesars of the New Rome the existence of the Russian state, from its creation in the ninth century, was an important fact which entered permanently into the calculations of their foreign policy. The contrast between the presence of political relations in one case and their almost complete absence in the other is reflected in the contrast between the circumstances of the victory of Christianity in Russia and in Ireland. In Russia the faith of the Empire made, as it were, a solemn entry through the public portals of the State; in Ireland it entered privately through postern gates, and conquered from within. In Russia it was imposed upon his subjects by their prince Vladimir, who at the same time married a sister of the Roman Augusti; in Ireland it was only tolerated, when its success had begun, by the chief king, whose very name most probably never fell upon the ears of the Augustus at Ravenna. But in both cases the introduction of the religion was only a part, though the most important and effective part, of a wider influence diffused from the Empire.

The great question with which Loigaire had to deal was the spread of Christianity in his dominion, a question which confronted barbarian kings just as it confronted Roman Emperors, and might be as embarrassing and critical for Loigaire in his small sphere as it had proved for the ecumenical statesmen Diocletian and Constantine. It is clear that in the days of Theodosius II. the moment had come when the High King of Ireland was constrained to adopt a definite attitude. If, as seems possible, it was in the south of Ireland, in the realms of Leinster and Munster, that this religion had hitherto made most progress, then, so long as it was tolerated by the sovereigns of those kingdoms, the High King might ignore it. But once it began to spread sensibly in his own immediate kingdom of Meath, as king of Meath he could not ignore what in other parts of Ireland the lord of all Ireland might pass over; the time had come when he had to decide whether he would oppose or recognise Christian communities and Christian priests.

For most barbarian kings this question would be equivalent to another, Shall I myself adopt the foreign faith? It argues in Loigaire exceptional ability and objectivity of vision that he was capable of separating his own personal view from his kingly policy. He was not drawn himself to the creed of

Christ; he held fast to the pagan faith and customs of his fathers; but this did not hinder him from recognising the great and growing strength of the religion which had overflowed from the Empire into his island. He saw that it had already taken root, and we may be certain that its close identification with the great Empire, the union of Christ with Caesar, was an imposing argument.[3] But if King Loigaire resolved on a policy of toleration, and was ultimately prepared to "regularise" the position of the Christian clerics, it is not unlikely that at first he may have been inclined to adopt a different attitude. It must have been difficult for him to withstand the influence of the Druids, who naturally put forth all their efforts to check the advance of the dangerous doctrine which had come from over seas to destroy their profession, their religion, and their gods. Tradition recorded their prophecies that the new faith, if it were admitted, would subvert kings and kingdoms. In legend, as we shall see, Loigaire appears as following the counsels of his Druids, resolving to slay Patrick, and yielding only when the sorcery of the Christian proved stronger than the sorcery of the heathen magicians. It is possible that this tale may reflect facts in so far as Loigaire may have been inclined to persecute before he adopted his policy of even-handed toleration. We must not leave out of our account the circumstance that, as in the case of Frankish Chlodwig and English Ethelbert, there were probably friends of the Christian religion in the king's own household.

Ethelbert indeed was not like Loigaire. He, too, began with the resolve to remain true to his own gods, while he granted licence to the priests of his wife's creed to do their will in his realm. Before two years had passed, however, the

English king forsook the old way himself and was initiated in the Christian rites, while the Irish king never abandoned the faith of his fathers. But Ethelbert's wife, like Chlodwig's, was a Christian, while of Loigaire's we cannot say what gods she worshipped; we have only the record that she was a native of Britain, and, for all we know, she may have been dead when Patrick arrived on the scene. Yet the fact that he had a British wife may supply a point of contact between the Irish king and the Empire and help to explain his tolerant attitude to the Roman religion. But he had also a British daughter-in-law, and here, if the main facts of the following story are true, we may fairly seek a co-operating influence.

In mid Meath, on the banks of the river Boyne, where it winds in one of its loveliest curves through the plain to the west of the royal hill of Tara, a small Christian settlement arose, perhaps soon after Patrick's arrival in Ireland. The place was called the "ford of the alder," and the name of the tree, Trim, still clings to it. In this spot Fedilmid, son of King Loigaire, had his dwelling, and his wife was a lady of Britain, who, if not already a Christian, must have had some knowledge of the established religion of the Empire of which Britain was still in name a province. Trim, according to its own tradition, was the scene of one of Patrick's most important successes.

The naive story relates that Lomman, one of Patrick's British fellow-workers, sailed up the Boyne and landed at the Ford of the Alder. In the morning Fedilmid's young son, Fortchernn,[4] sallied forth and found Lomman reading the Gospel. Immediately the boy believed and was baptized, and remained with Lomman till his mother came out to seek him. She was delighted to meet a fellow-countryman, and she, too, believed and returned to her house and told Fedilmid all that had befallen their son. Then Fedilmid conversed with Lomman in the British tongue, and believed with all his household. He consigned Fortchernn to the care of Lomman, to be his pupil and spiritual foster-child, and made a donation of his estate at Trim to Patrick and Lomman and Fortchernn.

Though the details of this story cannot be taken literally, it may probably preserve correctly some of the main facts — that Fortchernn became a pupil of Lomman and embraced the spiritual life; that Fedilmid made the donation, and that the British princess played a part in the episode. But tales of this kind are prone to represent circumstances, which were really due to design, as the effect of chance. It is possible that the British princess was already a Christian, and that, just as Augustine travelled to Kent by the invitation of its Gallic queen, so Lomman rowed to Trim at the call of its British mistress. In any case we may be sure that Lomman's coming to the Ford of the Alder was not fortuitous, but was arranged by him and Patrick with forethought and purpose. The result was of high importance. It gave Patrick a strong position and prestige in Meath by establishing a Christian community with which the son and grandson of the High King were so closely associated.

§2. *Legend of Patrick's Contest with the Druids*

The bitter hostility of the Druids and the relations of Loigaire to Patrick were worked up by Irish imagination into a legend which ushers in the saint upon the scene of his work with great spectacular effect. The story represents him as resolving to celebrate the first Easter after his landing in Ireland on the hill of Slane, which rises high above the left bank of the Boyne at about twelve miles from its mouth. On the night of Easter eve he and his companions lit the Paschal fire, and on that selfsame night it so chanced that the King of Ireland held a high and solemn festival in his palace at Tara where the kings and nobles of the land gathered together. It was the custom that on that night of the year no fire should be lit until a fire had been kindled with solemn ritual in the royal house. Suddenly the company assembled at Tara saw a light shining across the plain of Breg from the hill of Slane.[5] King Loigaire, in surprise and alarm, consulted his magicians, and they said, "O king, unless this fire which you see be quenched this same night, it will never be quenched; and the kindler of it will overcome us all and seduce all the folk of your realm." And the king replied, "It shall not be, but we will go to see the issue of the matter, and we will put to death those who do such sin against our kingdom." So he had nine chariots yoked, and, with the queen and his two chief sorcerers and others, he drove through the night over the plain of Breg. And in order to win magic power over them who had kindled the fire, they wheeled lefthandwise, or contrariwise to the sun's course. And the magicians arranged with the king that he should not go up to the place where the fire was kindled, lest he should afterwards worship the kindler thereof, but that the offender should be summoned to the king's presence at some distance from the fire, and the magicians should converse with him.

Map of the Kingdoms of
MEATH AND CONNAUGHT.

DALARADIA

Cuailgne

Conaille Muirthemni

Inber Colpthi

Inis Patraic

BREG

Domnach Sechnaill
(Dunshaughlin)

MAG

Temair
(Tara)

Mag Life

LAIGIN

Tailtiu (Teltown)
o Domnach Patraic
(Donaghpatrick)

Slane (R. Blackwater)

Boand (R. Boyne)

Cenondas (Kells)

Ath Truimm
(Trim)

MIDE

Tlacht'ga

Uisnech

Tethba

Tethba

Slige (R. Brosna)

L. Allen

Mag Slecht

L. Arrow

I. Ce

L. Gill

o Druim Lias
(Drumlease)

Shencua
(Shancoe)

Tammnach
(Tawnagh)
o Echenach
(Aghanagh)

TIR AILILL

TIR FIACHRACH

L. Tecet

Mag Airthic

L. Bidberg

Mag Luirg

Cell Moro

Mag Gliss

Ailfinn
(Elphin) o

Mag Caireth

Mag Rein

L. Ribh
(L. Ree)

R. Shannon

Rath Crochan

o Bastic

Sruthair

o (Oran)

Succa (R. Suck)

MAG AI

Cassel
o Killaspugbrone

Domnach Mor
(Crosspatrick)

TIR FIACHRACH

L. Mov

Muad

TIR AMOLNGID

FOCHLAD

MAG
DOMNON

MUIRISCC

L. Conon

Luigne

Mruad

L. Tecet

Mag Talraeu

Mag Aige
(Croagh Patrick)

Ached Fobuir
(Aghagower)

Cruachan Aige

Conmaicne

Mag Caeri

O Crannet

ARAIGNE

Comnaicne
ni Cuil Tulat

L. Mask

CONACHT

L. Corrib

R & R Clark Ltd Edinburgh.

So the company dismounted out of range of the fire, and Patrick was summoned. And the sorcerers said, "Let none arise at his coming, for whoever rises will afterwards worship him." When Patrick came and saw the chariots and horses, he quoted the words of the Psalmist, "Some in chariots and some on horses, but we in the name of the Lord." One of the company, and one only—his name was Ere—rose up when Patrick appeared, and he was converted and Patrick blessed him (and he was afterwards buried at Slane). Then the sorcerers and Patrick began to converse and dispute; and Lochru, one of the enchanters, uttered strong words against the Christian faith. And Patrick, looking grimly at him, prayed to God that the blasphemer should be flung into the air and dashed to the ground. And so it befell. Lochru was lifted upwards and fell upon a stone, so that his head was dashed in pieces. Then the king was wroth and said, "Lay hands upon the fellow." And Patrick, seeing the heathen about to attack him, cried in a loud voice, "Let God arise, and let his enemies be scattered." Then a great darkness fell and the earth quaked, and in the tumult the heathen fell upon each other, and the horses fled over the plain, and of all that company only the king and queen, and Lucetmael, the other sorcerer, and a few others survived. Then the queen went to Patrick and besought him, saying, "O mighty and just man, do not destroy the king! He will come and kneel and worship your god." And the king, constrained by fear, bent his knee to Patrick and pretended to worship God. But afterwards he bade Patrick to him, purposing to slay him; but Patrick knew his thoughts, and he went before the king with his eight companions, one of whom was a boy. But as the king counted them, lo! they were no longer there, but he saw in the distance eight deer and a fawn making for the wilds. And the king returned in the morning twilight to Tara, disheartened and ashamed.

The framers of this legend had an instinct for scenic effect. The bold and brilliant idea of the first Easter fire flashing defiance across the plain of Meath to the heathen powers of Tara, and the vision of the king with his queen and sorcerers setting forth from their palace in the depth of night with chariots and horses, and careering over the plain, as Ailill and Maeve of pagan story might have suddenly driven in headlong course against the Hound of Ulaid, is a picture not unworthy of the best of those nameless story-makers who in all lands, working one cannot tell where or how, transfigure the facts of history. The calendar is disregarded. The idea is that Easter is to replace Beltane, the Christian to overcome the heathen fire; and it is a matter of no import that the day of Beltane was the first day of summer, which could never fall on Easter Eve.[6] But incongruous though the circumstances are, the scene is well conceived to express the triumph of the new faith, and certain general historical facts are embodied, namely, the hostility of the Druids and the personal distaste of the king for the foreign creed.

And the imaginary coincidence of the pagan with the Christian festival has a historical interest of its own. Down to modern times we find the ancient heathen customs of Europe observed in different countries on different days. In some regions they were transferred to Christian feasts like Easter and Pentecost, elsewhere the old heathen days were preserved. When the old practice was adapted to the frame of the new faith, the change was silent and unrecorded, but this Irish legend, by its impossible junction of the two festivals, may be said to embody unconsciously a record of such a change. We can detect here, in the very act as it were, the process by which pagan superstitions which insisted on surviving were sometimes adopted into the Christian calendar.

The story has a sequel which tells how Patrick strove with the other enchanter. On the morrow, that is, Easter day, Loigaire, with kings and princes and nobles, was feasting in his palace, when Patrick with five companions suddenly appeared among them, though the door was shut.[7] He came to preach the Word, and the king invited him to sit at meat. Lucetmael, the Druid, in order to prove him, poured a noxious drop into the cup of Patrick, and the saint blessed the cup, and the liquor was frozen to ice, except the drop of poison, which remained liquid, and fell out when the cup was turned upside down. Then he blessed the cup again, and the drink returned into its natural state.

Then the magician said, "Let us work miracles on the plain; let us bring down snow upon the land." Patrick said, "I will not bring down aught against the will of God." And the magician by his incantations brought snow waist-high upon the plain. "Now remove it," said the saint. "I cannot," said the Druid, "till this hour upon the morrow." "You can do evil," answered the saint, "but not good," and he blessed the plain, and the snow vanished without rain, or mist, or wind. And all applauded and marvelled. Then in the same way the Druid brought darkness down over the plain, but he could not dissipate it, and Patrick dissipated it.

Then said the king, "Dip your books in the water, and we will worship him whose books come out unspoiled." Patrick was willing to accept this test, but the sorcerer refused on the ground that Patrick worshipped water as a god, meaning its use in baptism. Then the king proposed the same test with fire instead of water; but the Druid said, "No, this man worships fire and water alternately." But all these parleyings were only preliminary, leading up to the main issue, which is closely connected with the events of the previous night. Patrick proposed an ordeal, which was accepted. His pupil Benignus and the magician were placed in a hut built half of green and half of dry wood. Benignus, clothed in the magician's garment, was placed in the dry part, and Lucetmael, wearing the garment of Patrick, in the green part. And the hut was set on fire in the presence of all. Then Patrick prayed, and the fire consumed the magician, leaving Patrick's robe unburnt, but it did not hurt Benignus, though it burnt the magician's robe from about him. Then Loigaire was fain to kill Patrick, but he was afraid.

Having discerned that one of the motives of the whole legend is the adoption in the Christian Church, in connexion with the Easter festival, of those fire-customs and sun-charms which were associated throughout Celtic, as throughout Teutonic, Europe with certain days in spring or early summer, we can hardly avoid recognising in this ordeal a memory of the custom of burning a victim on those days. This victim was thought to represent the spirit of vegetation, and its ashes were carried forth and scattered in the fields to make them fruitful. Originally the victim was human, but as time went on, either a mock victim, such as a straw man, was substituted, or he who was chosen to die and decked out for sacrifice was rescued at the brink of the fire. In the Eiffel country, by the Rhine, for instance, the custom was long maintained of heaping brushwood round a tall beech-tree, and forming a framework known as the "burg" or the "hut," and a straw man was sometimes burned in it. We can hardly doubt that the chief ceremonial of the Beltane celebration, the burning of the spirit of growth—whether represented by a man or by a mock man, whether in a dress of leaves or in a framework of green or dry wood—was the motive which suggested the story of this ordeal. In the story the motive has lost its particular significance, and but for its connexion with the opposition between Easter and Beltane might escape detection.

The envelopment of a motive of somewhat the same kind in a setting which purposes to be historical, and in which the motive entirely loses its meaning, has an instructive parallel in the famous story of the funeral pyre of king Croesus. The fundamental motive of that story is the burning of the god Sandan, but the incident has been wrought into a historical context so as to disguise its origin, and the tale was largely accepted as literal fact. But Cyrus was as innocent of dooming his defeated foe to a cruel death as Patrick was of burning his Druid rival. In both cases the true victims of the legendary flames were spirits of popular imagination.

The story bears the stamp of an early origin. It is a common fallacy that legends attach themselves to a figure only after a long lapse of time, and that the antiquity of biographies may always be measured by the presence or absence of miracles. The truth is that those men who are destined to become the subjects of myth evoke the mythopoeic instinct in their fellows while they are still alive, or before they are cold in their graves. When once the tale is set rolling it may gather up as time goes on many conventional and insignificant accretions of fiction, and the presence or absence of these may indeed be a guide in determining the age of a document. But the myths which are significant and characteristic are nearly contemporary; they arise within the radius of the personality to which they relate. The tale of Patrick's first Easter in Ireland and his dealings with the king is eminently a creation of this kind.

In this legend of Patrick's dealings with the High King there is one implication which harmonises with other records,[8] and which, we cannot doubt, reflects, while it distorts, a fact. Patrick visited Loigaire in his palace at Tara, but he went as a guest in peace, not as a hostile magician and a destroyer of life. The position which the Christian creed had won rendered a conference no less desirable for the High King than for the bishop who represented the Church of the Empire. Loigaire agreed to protect Patrick in his own kingdom, though he resisted any attempts that were made to convert him. No cross should be raised over his sepulchre; he should be buried, like his forefathers, standing and accoutred in his arms.

But the place of the Christian communities in the society of Ireland, their rights and obligations, and the modifications of existing customs and laws which the principles and doctrines of their religion demanded, raised questions which could not well be settled except in a general conclave of the kings and chief men of the island. Now it was a custom of the

High Kings to hold occasionally a great celebration, called the Feast of Tara, to which the under-kings were invited. It was an opportunity for discussing the common affairs of the realm. Such an occasion is evidently contemplated in the legend, and the Annals record that a Feast of Tara was held towards the close of Loigaire's reign. It is therefore possible that at such an assembly the religious question was marked as a subject of deliberation, and the bishop was invited to be present. If so, the general issue of the debate must have been that Christian communities were recognised as social units on the same footing as families, but that Christian principles could not alter the general principles of Irish law. This brings us to the chief monument of Loigaire's reign, the legal code, the construction of which may well have been discussed and resolved on at one of the general assemblages at Tara.

§3. *Loigaire's Code*

Loigaire did for Ireland what Euric did for the Visigoths, Gundobad for the Burgundians, Chlodwig for the Salian Franks; and we have already observed that to him probably, as to them, the idea of compiling a written legal code came from the Roman Empire. The *Senchus Mór,* as the code was called, has not come down in its primitive form; it has been remodelled, worked over, and overlaid with additions by subsequent lawyers; but a critical examination of the evidence leaves little room for doubt that in its original shape it was, as tradition held, composed under the auspices of Loigaire. As it was to be valid for Ireland, and not merely for Meath, it was necessary for the High King to act in consort with the provincial kings, and tradition mentions as his coadjutors Core, king of Munster, and Daire of Orior.

If the view is right that the initiation of such a code was due to the influence of Roman ideas, it would be not unnatural or surprising that the Christian bishop and Roman citizen, who represented more than any other man in Ireland the ideas of Roman civilisation, should have been consulted, though the construction of the law-book was a matter for native experts. But there was another reason why Patrick would naturally have been taken into the counsels of the kings and lawyers. The spread of Christianity and the foundation of Christian communities throughout the land rendered it imperative for the secular authorities to define the status of the clergy and fix the law which should be binding on all. A new society had been established, recognising laws of its own, which differed from the laws of the country; and this threatened to create a double system, which would have been fatal to order. Either the spirit of the Mosaic law must be allowed to transform the ancient customs of the land, or the Christians must resign themselves to living under principles opposed to ecclesiastical teaching.

It is possible that Patrick made an attempt to revolutionise the Irish system of dealing with cases of manslaughter, to abolish the customs of composition by fine and private re-taliation, and make it an offence punishable by death. But if he made such an attempt it was unsuccessful, and it would probably have received little support from his native con-verts. The principle of primitive societies that bloodshedding was a private offence which could be atoned for by payment of a composition—a principle which Greek societies were discarding in the seventh century B.C.—prevailed in Ireland so long as Ireland was independent, and the Irish Church was perfectly content.

Among the experts who are said to have taken part in compiling the code was the poet Dubthach, of Leinster, who is said to have been one of the most eminent poets in the reign of Loigaire. Tradition says that he became a Christian, and his pupil Fíacc, whom he had trained in the art of poetry, was consecrated a bishop by Patrick. Of the poets of Ireland at this early age we know nothing. One wonders what manner of poems were sung by that bard whose sepulchral stone, old but of unknown age, has preserved his bare name and calling, written in the character which the Irish of those days used to inscribe upon their tombstones: VELITAS LUGUTTI, "(This is the tomb) of the poet Lugut."[9] The poets were men of dignity and consequence in the society of their tribes and country. They were not only poets but judges, for they possessed the legal lore which was perhaps preserved in poetical form. The administration of justice depended on their knowledge; their arbitrations were the substitute for a court of justice. Such was the position of Dubthach, lawyer at once and poet, like Charondas of Catana, whose laws, cast in poetical form, were sung, we are told, at banquets. He was a native of Leinster, and if he was one of the commission which drew up the *Senchus Mór*, we may take it that he represented that kingdom, for the name of the King of Leinster, Loigaire's enemy, does not appear.

The legend of Patrick's visit to Tara, when he entered through closed doors, relates that when he appeared in the hall Dubthach alone of the company rose from his seat to salute the stranger. This seems to be a genuine fragment of tradition. That there had been a friendship between Patrick and Dubthach was believed in later times at Sletty, in Leinster, of which Fíacc, pupil of Dubthach, was the first bishop.

§4. *Ecclesiastical Foundations in Meath*

The early traditions of Patrick's work in founding new communities claim our notice, for though we cannot control them in any particular case, the probability is that many of them have a basis in fact, and collectively they illustrate this side of his activity.

Within Loigaire's own immediate kingdom not a few churches claimed to have been founded by Patrick, one or two of them in the neighbourhood of the royal hill. But though the names of the places where these churches were built are recorded, they are in most cases for us mere names; the sites cannot be identified, or can only be guessed at. In a few places in the land of Meath we can localise the literary traditions. We may begin with a church which was founded not by the bishop himself, but by a disciple and, it was believed, a relative. Not far south from Tara lies Dunshaughlin, and the name, which represents[10] Domnach Sechnaill, "the church of Sechnall," is supposed to preserve the name of Sechnall or Secundinus, said to have been Patrick's nephew. Here Secundinus is related to have composed the first Latin hymn that was composed in Ireland, and the theme of the hymn was the apostolic work of his master. This hymn is undoubtedly contemporary, and there is no reason either to deny or to assert the authenticity of the tradition which ascribes it to

Secundinus, but there are considerations which make it very difficult to accept his alleged relationship to Patrick. It is composed in trochaic rhythm, but with almost complete disregard of metrical quantity, and its twenty-three quatrains begin with the successive letters of the alphabet. Literary merit it has none, and the historian deplores that, instead of singing the general praises of Patrick's virtues and weaving round him a mesh of religious phrases describing his work as pastor, messenger, and preacher, the author had thought well to mention some of his particular actions. But the hymn has its value. It is among the earliest memorials that we possess of his work; and if it was composed by Secundinus, it was written before Patrick had been fourteen years in Ireland, and is thus older than the greater memorial which he wrote himself before he died. And the writer may have derived his inspiration from Patrick's own impressions about his work. We may suspect that some of the verses echo words which had fallen from Patrick's lips in the hearing of his disciple, as when the master is compared to Paul,[11] or described as a fisherman setting his nets for the heathen, or called the light of the world, or a witness of God *in lege catholica*. But Secundinus, if he was the hymnographer, did not live to see the fuller realisation of Patrick's claims to the fulsome laudations of his hymn. The disciple died long before the master had finished his" perfect life."[12]

In another district of Meath, Donagh-Patrick, near the banks of the Blackwater, seems to mark a spot associated with an important success of the apostle. Here Conall, son of Niall, and brother of king Loigaire, had his dwelling, still marked by the foundations of an ancient fort, and he was less deaf than his greater brother to the persuasions of Patrick's teaching. He submitted to the rite of baptism, and he granted a place, close to his own house, for the building of a church. Patrick measured out the ground, and a church of unusual size arose, twenty yards from end to end, and it was known as the Great Church of Patrick. Such was the scale of the early houses of Christian worship in Ireland.

The conversion of Conall was an important achievement, but it is related that there were other sons of Niall, who were so bitterly adverse to the new doctrine, that they were fain to take the life of its teacher. Not far from the place where he won the friendship of Conall, Patrick had been in danger of his life at the hands of Coirpre, Conall's brother. At a little distance above the confluence of the Blackwater with the Boyne, the village of Telltown recalls the memory of Taillte,[13] a place of great note and fame in ancient Meath. Here a fair was held and a feast celebrated at the beginning of autumn, and people gathered together to witness the games which were held there, perhaps under the presidency of the High King. The record of the visit of Patrick to Taillte mentions the games as the "royal agon," and the Greek word sends our thoughts to those more illustrious contests which were held at the same season of the year on the banks of the Alpheus in honour of Zeus. It is not clear whether Patrick is supposed to have timed his visit to see and denounce the heathen usages of the festival. Perhaps he would have avoided such an occasion with the same discretion which Otto, the apostle of the Pomeranians, exercised when he waited outside the town of Pyritz till the pagan folk had finished the celebration of a religious feast.[14] The story is that Coirpre, son of King

Niall, wished to put Patrick to death at Taillte, and scourged his servants because they would not betray their master into his hands.

But if the bishop was in danger from a son of Niall at Taillte, he is said to have fared worse at the hands of a grandson of Niall[15] at another place of high repute in the kingdom of Meath. The hill of Uisnech, in south-western Meath, was believed to mark the centre of the island, and was a scene of pagan worship. Patrick visited the hill town, and a stone known as the "stone of Coithrige"—perhaps a sacred stone on which he inscribed a cross—commemorated his name and his visit. The stone has disappeared, but the traveller is reminded of it by the stone enclosure which is known as "St Patrick's bed." While he was there, a grandson of Niall slew some of his foreign companions. Patrick cursed both this man and Coirpre, and foretold that no king should ever spring from their seed, but that their posterity would serve the posterity of their brethren. Tradition consistently represents Patrick as finding in malediction an instrument not to be disdained.

It is recorded that, proceeding from Donagh-Patrick up the Blackwater, he came to the Ford of the Quern,[16] and planted there another Christian settlement. This place was probably near the old town of Kells, then called Cenondae. Unlike Trim, Kells has some traces of the early age of Christian Ireland, though nothing that can claim association with the age of Patrick. The ancient stone house which is preserved there, is connected by tradition with the name of the great saint who a hundred years after Patrick's death went forth from Ireland to convert north Britain.[17]

Some churches are said to have been established by Patrick in the north-western region of Meath, which was known by a name, now obsolete, as the kingdom of the two Tethbias.[18] The river Ethne, which is now pronounced Inny, flows through this region to contribute its waters to a swelling of the Shannon, and divides it into two parts, the northern and the southern Tethbia. Perhaps the only place here that we have any ground for associating with Patrick is Granard. We are told that from the hill of Granard he pointed out to one of his followers the spot where a church should be founded. This church, Cell Raithin, may have been the origin of the settlement which grew into the town of Granard. Among the inmates of the monastery established here is said to have been one who had a specially interesting connexion with Patrick's life. Gosact, described as the son of his old master, was, according to the tradition, here ordained a priest by the captive stranger who had once kept his father's droves. There cannot be any reasonable doubt that the tomb of Gosact was in later times to be seen at Granard, and that the tradition of the place represented him as the son of Miliucc. Nor should we have any good reason to question that Gosact, who was buried there, was a son of Miliucc. But we have seen grounds for believing that the story of Patrick's servitude under Miliucc of Dalaradia was an error; and it would follow that Gosact, son of Miliucc, was not the son of Patrick's master. Nevertheless, Gosact may have been connected with the years of bondage, and may perhaps supply us with the clue which we desire for explaining how it came about that it ever occurred to any one to place the scene of the captivity in the land of Miliucc. In the earliest notice of Gosact that is preserved, he is said to have been fostered by Patrick during the servitude of seven years. This suggests the conjecture that, in conformity with a custom which prevailed in Ireland, Miliucc had sent his son from home to be brought up by Patrick's master in Connaught, and that through this accident, happening at the time of the captivity, Patrick had associated with Gosact. The record of this bond between Patrick and Miliucc's son might have originated the error that Miliucc was Patrick's master.

It is said that, having done what he could do towards planting his religion here and there in Tethbia, Patrick bent his steps northward to one of the chief strongholds and sanctuaries of pagan worship in Ireland. In the plain of Slecht, in a region which belonged then to the kingdom of Connaught, but falls now within the province of Ulster, there was a famous idol. It was apparently a stone, covered with silver and gold, standing in a sacred circuit, surrounded by twelve pillar stones. This idol was known as Cenn Cruaich or Crom Cruaich, and it has been suggested that a fossilised memory of the same worship is found in a name among the British Celts beyond the sea, Pennicrucium. We may suspect that either later generations exalted unduly the importance of the precinct in Mag Slecht as a national centre of religion, or that its importance had dwindled before the days of Patrick. It was told in later times that the firstlings, even of human offspring, used to be offered to this idol, in order to secure a plenteous yield of corn and milk, and that the High Kings of Ireland themselves used to come at the beginning of winter to do worship in the plain of Slecht. If the cult in that plain possessed such national significance as was in later times

believed, it would have been one of Patrick's greatest feats if
he assaulted and conquered the power of heathendom in one
of its chief fastnesses. The story tells, with a simplicity which
defeats itself, that he came and struck down the idol with his
staff. If this was done, if the golden pillar of the older god
was thus cast down by the servant of the new divinity, it must
have been done with the consent of secular powers. It would
thus have marked, perhaps more than any other single event,
the formal success of Christian aggression against the pagan
spirit of Ireland, and it would inevitably have stood out in
the earliest records as one of the decisive victories, if not the
supreme triumph. The blow struck by Patrick at the stone of
Mag Slecht would be as the stroke of Boniface at the oak of
Geismar. The fall of Cenn Cruaich should be as illustrious in
the story of the spreading of Christianity in the island of the
Scots as was the fall of the Irmin pillar on a Westphalian hill
in the advance of Christendom from the Rhine to the Elbe,
under the banner of Charles the Great. The apostle of the
Irish might as justly and proudly have sent some fragment
of the fallen image to the Roman pontiff, a trophy of the
victory of their faith, as in a later age the apostle of the Baltic
Slavs sent to Rome the three-headed god which he took from
the temple of Stettin to show the head of the Church how
a new land was being won for Christ. But the truth is that
the episode of Cenn Cruaich, though the incident rests on
an ancient tradition, held no prominent place in the oldest
records. Perhaps we shall be near the mark if we infer that the
story is based on a genuine fact, but that the later accounts
impute to it a significance which it did not possess.[19] We may
suppose that the worship of the idol was of interest only to

the surrounding regions, and had no national import for the whole island. If Patrick went to the place and with the help of secular authority suppressed the worship and cast down the god, it was simply one of his local successes, one of many victories in his struggle with heathenism, not a crowning or typical triumph.

VII

IN CONNAUGHT

IT is uncertain how long Patrick had been in the island before he set forth to accomplish the thing which had been the dream of his life, the preaching of his gospel in the western parts of Connaught, *ubi nemo ultra erat,* by the utmost margin of European land. We remember how the cry of the children of Fochlad, heard in the visions of the night, was the supreme call which he felt as irresistible. And although his outlook must have widened as he came face to face with facts, and new tasks of great worth and moment, presenting themselves, transformed and enlarged the conception of his work as he had originally grasped it, we cannot doubt that to bear light to the forest of Fochlad was the most cherished wish of his heart. Nor is it likely that, however much he found to do in Ulidia and Meath, he would have deferred this purpose long, unless some grave obstacle had constrained him to delay. The necessary condition of success was the consent of the king of the land; the decisive hindrance would have been his disapprobation and opposition.

Now there was one district close to the woods of Fochlad where Patrick was unable to fulfil his wishes till after the lapse of thirteen or fourteen years. This was the land of Amolngaid, in north Mayo, the land which is still called by that king's name—Tír Amolngid, which is pronounced Tirawley. It was not till after his death that the Christian bishop visited those regions, and it may be inferred, perhaps, that Amolngaid could not be persuaded to look with favour on the strange religion which his sons afterwards accepted. According to the common view, the forest of Fochlad was restricted to this corner of Connaught, and in that case Patrick's fulfilment of his original purpose would have been thus long delayed. But it has been pointed out in a previous chapter that Fochlad had possibly a wider compass, stretching across Mayo towards the neighbourhood of Murrisk, and that the scene of Patrick's bondage was in that neighbourhood. If so, our records allow us to suppose, though certainty cannot be attained, that he may have visited the southern limits of Fochlad at an earlier period. We are told that he crossed the Shannon and visited Connaught three times. One of these occasions was shortly after the death of king Amolngaid;[1] but one or both of the other visits may have been earlier, and on such an earlier occasion he may have made his way to the region which he had known of old as a bondslave. In our records, events which belong to different journeys are thrown together, and it is not possible, except at some particular points, to distinguish them; but this chronological uncertainty will not seriously affect the general view of Patrick's labours in Connaught as remembered there. In the following account of some of his acts it is assumed that his first two journeys were in the lifetime of Amolngaid; but while this assumption is adopted for the purpose of the narrative, it will be understood that it is only tentative.

The field of Patrick's work in his first journey beyond the Shannon seems to have been, partly, in the land of the children of Ailill. Their country covered a large part of the county of Sligo, and perhaps extended southward into Roscommon to the neighbourhood of Elphin. As in the case of other Irish kingdoms, its memory is still preserved in the name of a small portion of its original compass. The barony of Tir-errill is a remnant of the land of Ailill, son of king Eochaidh, and brother of king Niall.

In the north of this kingdom, on the west side of Lough Arrow, Patrick founded a church in a district which still bears the old name of Aghanagh; and east of the same lake, at the extreme border of Tirerrill, the parish of Shancoe enables us to fix the whereabouts of another church which he established at Senchua. There is a curious piece of evidence which suggests that Christianity had already made an attempt to win a footing in these regions. When Patrick ordained[2] a certain Ailbe, who belonged to the family of Ailill, to the rank of priest, he told him of the existence of a "wonderful" subterranean stone altar in the Mountain of the Children of Ailill. There were four glass chalices at the four corners of the altar, and Patrick warned Ailbe to beware of breaking the edges of the excavation. As Shancoe was Ailbe's church, we are entitled to infer that the altar was somewhere in the Bralieve hills, which are in that district.[3] It is clear that, if the tradition is genuine, Patrick had seen the place himself, and the story implies that it was not he who had set the altar in the lonely spot on the mountains, but that it had been used in older days and abandoned.

No commemorative name has survived to mark the place of another church in the same regions which owed its origin to Patrick, the Cell Angle;[4] but what seems to have been the most important foundation of all was farther north, in the parish of Tawnagh,[5] still called as it was called when he first gave it a place on the ecclesiastical map of Ireland.

It seems probable that in his first journey Patrick also visited the north of Sligo, and consecrated Brón bishop for a church founded at Caissel-ire. This place was on the sea-shore, under the massive hill of Knocknaree, which dominates on the west the modern town of Sligo, and the name Kill-espug-brone[6] still preserves the memory of the fifth-century bishop.

He also worked in the regions south of Lake Gara, where Sachall, whom we shall presently meet as a bishop, became his pupil. Thence he may have journeyed southward through the plains and wilds of Kerry,[7] founding some churches on his way, till he came to the lake country on the confines of Mayo and Galway. Then he turned westward through Carra and founded the church of Achad-fobuir. The old name has clung to the place—Aghagower, and in ancient times it had ecclesiastical importance.[8] It marks clearly a stage in the apostle's progress to the famous mountain to which his visit gave a new name.

If we are right in supposing that this was the region in which Patrick spent the years of his captivity, that this was the home of the children of Fochlad who called to him in his dreams, the church of Aghagower would possess a singular interest among all the churches which he founded in Ireland, as fulfilling the wish which had first impelled him to make the great resolve of his life. Here he revisited the scenes where he had herded his master's flocks and prayed at night in the woods in snow and rain. Here he climbed again the mountain which he mentions in his own description of the days of bondage, and which was always henceforward to be linked with his own name. Crochan Aigli rises high and prominent on the north shore of the wild desolate promontory, which is girt on three sides by the sea, and is known as the "sea-land."[9] To the summit of this peak Patrick is said to have retired for lonely contemplation and prayer. It is said that he remained there fasting forty days and forty nights, like the Jewish teachers, Moses, Elias, and Jesus. It may be thought that this report arose from the pious inclination of later admirers to seek in his life similitudes to the lives of Moses and other holy men of the Christian Scriptures. But it is conceivable that the similitude was designed by Patrick himself. It is not unlikely that, if he desired a season of isolation to commune with his own soul and meditate on things invisible, he should have fixed the term of his retreat by the highest examples. The forty days and forty nights may be the literal truth, and may have helped to move the imagination of his disciples to create a legend. For in after days men pictured the saint encompassed by the company of the saints of Ireland. God said to the souls of the saints, not only of the dead and living, but of the still unborn, "Go up, O ye saints, to the top of the mountain which is higher[10] than all the other mountains of the west, and bless the folks of Ireland." Then the souls mounted, and they flitted round the lofty peak in the form of birds, darkening the air, so great was their multitude. Thus God heartened Patrick by revealing to him the fruit of his labours.

Ever since, this western mount has been associated with the foreign teacher, not only bearing his name, but drawing to it multitudes of pilgrims, who every year, as the anniversary of his death comes round, toil up the steep ascent of Croagh Patrick, imbued still with the same superstitious feelings which moved the minds of Christian and heathen, of clerk and lay alike, in the days of Patrick. The confined space of its summit is the one spot where we feel some assurance that we can stand literally in his footsteps and realise that, as we look southward over the desolate moors and tarns of Murrisk, northward across the bay to the hills of Burrishoole and Erris, and then westward beyond the islets to the spaces of the ocean, we are viewing a scene on which Patrick for many days looked forth with the bodily eye. But the spot has a greater interest if it is associated not only with the ground of solitary retreat in his later years, but with the servitude of his boyhood. For if this was so, the meditations on the mount were interfused with emotions intelligible to the children of reason, who do not understand the need of "saints" for fasting and prayer. It requires little imagination to realise in some sort what the man's feelings must have been when he returned to the places of his thraldom, conscious that he was now a "light among the Gentiles," and that his bitter captivity had led to such great results. It was a human as well as a saintly impulse to seek isolation on the mountain where he had first turned to thoughts of religion amidst the herds of his heathen lord.

In the case of what we may suppose to have been another and later journey in Connaught some genuine tradition of the line of advance appears to have been preserved. The bishop is said to have travelled westward through the southern corner of Leitrim to the banks of the Shannon. That river sweeps to the east below the town of the Rock,[11] and then, continuing its southward course, widens into a series of swellings, which, though small compared with the greater sheets of water into which it afterwards expands, are striking in their peculiar form. The stream flows through Lake Nanoge, Lake Tap, Lake Boderg, and Lake Bofin, but the special feature is the long arm of water which it flings south-westward, known as Lake Kilglass. The effect of this is that the river seems to bifurcate, and a promontory is formed by the true stream and Lake Bofin on the east, and by the blind water passage of Lake Kilglass on the west. It was to these river-lakes that Patrick bent his way, and the place of his crossing, though not designated by any name that is still used, is yet so clearly defined that we cannot mistake it, and can hardly doubt that the tradition is true. He first crossed over a river-swelling, and then found a second swelling in front of him, which he also passed. The only place in the course of the Shannon which satisfies these conditions is the place which has been described. When he was rowed across Lake Bofin, Patrick found himself on the water-girt promontory which is washed on the west by Lake Kilglass. In order to reach the district of Moyglass, which was his first destination, he took the shortest and most direct way, and crossed this second lake (perhaps near the modern Carnado Bridge) instead of making half-a-day's journey round its shores.

On reaching the other bank he was in the plain of Glass,[12] and here again we find that the name of a large district has been preserved in the name of a small part. The little townland of Moyglass is adjacent to Lake Tap, but the ancient plain of Glass extended, we may be confident, from the banks

of the river Shannon to the foot of the western hills, which
screen the river here from the great plain of Roscommon.
In this district the bishop established a Cell Mór or great
church, and his visit gave the place its abiding name. It can
be inferred that Patrick's church was close to the village of
Kilmore.

From the small plain of Glass Patrick made his way into
the great plain, known as Mag Ai, which extends over the
central part of the county of Roscommon. It is divided from
the Shannon by a screen of low hills, and only from some of
the ridges in the south of it can one descry, shimmering far
away, the waters of Lake Ree. When he crossed that chain of
hills, Patrick found himself in the land of the Corcu Ochland,
and he was welcomed by a certain Hono, who is described as
a Druid, and was evidently a man of wealth and influence.
There is good reason to believe that Hono was prepared for
Patrick's coming, for two of Patrick's disciples, Assicus and
his nephew Bitteus, along with Cipia, the mother of Bitteus,
were already with Hono when Patrick arrived. We may probably infer that Christianity had already made some way here,
and that, on Patrick's coming, no persuasions were necessary
to induce Hono to co-operate in founding a church and
monastery. They went together to the place which still bears
the name of the White Rock—Ailfinn, and there founded
together one of the most important of Patrick's ecclesiastical
foundations, which in later times, when the great dioceses
were formed, was to become the seat of a diocesan bishop.
The community of Elphin was to be under the headship
of Hono's descendants, but its first members were Assicus,
Betheus, and Cipia. Bishop Assicus, whose name has not

been forgotten at Elphin, was a skilful worker in bronze, and used to make for Patrick altars and cases for books. Square patens of his workmanship were long preserved as treasures at Armagh and at his own Elphin.

The next station of the bishop's journey was the seat of the kings of Connaught, the fortress of Crochan, famous in story. On one of the highest and broadest of the low ridges which mark the plain of Ái stood the royal palace, and though, as in the case of the other palaces of the kings of Ireland, no remains of the habitation survive except the earthen structure, it is something even to stand on the site of Rathcrochan, where queen Maeve and her lord lived—if they lived at all. Around the royal fort itself the ground is covered with other mounds and raths and memorials of ancient history, so that one can hardly fancy what appearance Crochan presented to Patrick. Near at hand was the place of sepulchres, to which the kings went down from their stronghold, as the kings of Mycenae went down from their citadel to the tombs below. In that field of the dead one red stone stands conspicuous to the present day, and the ill-certified tradition is that it marks the tomb of Dathi, the successor and nephew of Niall. If there were any truth in that tradition, the pillar would be an interesting link with the age of Patrick, for it would have been set up not many years before he visited the place.

Imagination peopled many spots in Ireland with supernatural beings—not only with fairies, but also with an earth-folk[13] that was once at least human, a conquered population who had formerly held the island, and, driven by invaders from the surface of the ground, had found new homes in chambered mounds, where they practised their magic crafts. But no spot was more closely associated with these fabled beings than the hill of Rathcrochan. On ground so alive with legend, in a place which stimulated fancy, it was hardly possible that the incident of Patrick's visit should be handed down in the sober colours of history or that it should escape the meshes of fable. But the legend-shaping instinct of some Christian poet wrought here with signal grace, and the story must have been invented not many decads of years after the visit to Rathcrochan.

Patrick, the tale tells, and the bishops who accompanied him, had assembled together at a fountain[14] near Rathcrochan to hold a council before sunrise, when two maidens came down, after the fashion of women, to wash at the fountain. They were the daughters of the High King of Ireland, and their names were Ethne the White and Fedelm the Red. They lived at Crochan, to be fostered and educated by two Druids, Mael and Caplait. These Druids had been deeply alarmed when they heard that Patrick was about to cross the Shannon, and by their sorceries they had brought down darkness and mist over the plain of Ai to hinder him from entering the land. The darkness of night prevailed for three days, but was dispelled by the saint's prayers.

When the princesses beheld the bishops and priests sitting round the fountain, they were amazed at their strange garb, and knew not what to think of them. Were they fairies—men of the *side*; or were they of the earth-folk—the Tuatha De Danann; or were they an illusion, an unreal vision? So they accosted and asked the strangers, "Whence have ye come, and where is your home?" And Patrick answered, "It were better for you to believe in the true God whom we worship than to ask questions about our race." Then the elder girl said, "Who is God, and where is God, and of whom is he God? Where is his dwelling? Has he sons and daughters, your God, and has he gold and silver? Is he immortal? Is he fair? Has his Son been fostered by many? Are his daughters dear to the men of the world, and fair in their eyes? Is he in heaven or in earth? in the sea, in the rivers, in the hill places, in the valleys? Tell us how we may know him, in whatwise he will appear. How is he discovered? Is he found in youth or in old age?"

To these greetings Patrick replied: "Our God is the God of all men, the God of heaven and earth, of sea and rivers, of sun and moon and stars, of the lofty mountain and the lowly valleys, the God above heaven and in heaven, and under heaven; he has his dwelling around heaven and earth and sea and all that in them is. He inspires all, he quickens all, he dominates all, he supports all. He lights the light of the sun; he furnishes the light of the night; he has made springs in the dry land, and has set stars to minister to the greater lights. He has a Son co-eternal with himself, and like unto himself. The Son is not younger than the Father, nor the Father older than the Son. And the Holy Spirit breathes in them. The Father, the Son, and the Spirit are not divided. I wish to unite you with the heavenly King, as ye are daughters of an earthly king. Believe."

With one voice and with one heart the two king's daughters said, "Tell us with all diligence how we may believe in the heavenly King that we may see Him face to face, and we will do as thou sayest." Patrick said, "Do ye believe that by baptism ye can cast away the sin of your father and mother?" They said, "We believe." "Do ye believe in repentance after sin?" "We believe." "Do ye believe in life after death?" "We believe." "Do ye believe in the resurrection in the day of Judgment?" "We believe." "Do ye believe in the unity of the Church?" "We believe."

Then Patrick baptized them in the fountain and placed a white veil on their heads, and they begged that they might behold the face of Christ. And Patrick said, "Until ye shall taste of death, ye cannot see the face of Christ, and unless ye shall receive the sacrifice." They answered, "Give us the sacrifice that we may see the Son, our bridegroom." And they received the Eucharist, and fell asleep in death. And they were placed in one bed, and their friends mourned them.

Then Caplait the Druid came, and Patrick preached to him, and he believed and became a monk. His brother Mael was wroth at his falling away, and hoped to recall him to the old faith, but on hearing Patrick's teaching he too became a Christian and his head was tonsured.

When the prescribed days of lamentation were over, the maidens were buried in a round tomb near the fountain. Their grave was dedicated to God and to Patrick and his heirs after him, and he constructed a church of earth in that place.

In this curious legend is embedded some matter of historical significance. In the first place we must treat the story of the brother Druids separately from the story of the maidens, for they are bound together only by an external link, and their motives are distinct. The motive of the legend of the two virgins who died in the hour of their conversion recurs in other tales, and the solid basis of fact was their tomb by the spring at Rathcrochan. At that tomb the story grew up that when they were baptized, their desire for the heavenly vision was fulfilled immediately by their death. This legend was then worked up artificially, and the dialogue was composed and written down in Irish, partly in verse. The freshness and simplicity, which are so striking, and some particular traits, justify us in surmising that this happened at an early date, within the first generation after the saint's death. The naive wonder of the maidens at the appearance of the clerks, the brief view which Patrick unfolds of the articles of his religion, the emphasis laid upon the unity of the Church, point to the conclusion that the story took shape when Patrick's ways of teaching, and the first impressions made upon pagans by the apostles of the new faith, were within the memory of the Church. The dialogue is artificial, for the questions of the damsels are arranged so as to lead up to the bishop's exposition of his creed. And, on the other hand, the baptismal questions of Patrick assume a knowledge on the part of the princesses which is inconsistent with their previous ignorance.

Now if we are right in the view that the legend originated at an early date and was cast into literary shape—at least before the end of the fifth century—we can hardly escape the inference that the maidens whose memory was preserved at Crochan were in truth daughters of Loigaire. Such an identification was not at all likely to have been invented by popular legend, nor by any recorder of Patrick's acts, living within a generation of his death. In sending children to be brought up away from their home, king Loigaire would have followed the general practice of the country, and that he should send them to the royal residence of Connaught would have been natural enough. The fathers of king Amolngaid and king Loigaire were brothers, and it would not be surprising that Loigaire should send his daughters to Rathcrochan to be educated by the Druids of Amolngaid.

But the episode of these brethren has an independent motive of its own. One brother, Mael, has an Irish name, designating the native tonsure, by which only the front part of the head was shaven from ear to ear; while Caplait, his fellow, has a Latin name (*Capillatus*), which signifies the removal of all the hair in the fashion already largely adopted in the western Empire, and subsequently known as the Roman tonsure. Both Druids alike were tonsured by Patrick according to the story; both alike, it is implied, wore the native tonsure before they were converted. The name *Caplait* could not have been applied to either till after his conversion. But when they became monks it applied equally to both, just as *Mael* was equally applicable to both when they were still pagans. Thus the story, taken literally, does not hang together, and the transparent names suggest that it arose from some circumstance connected with the Christian tonsure. Fortunately, the narrative supplies us with the clue. The writer who tells the tale observes that the incident gave rise to an Irish maxim, *cosmail Mael do Chaplait,* "Mael is like unto Caplait." It is manifest that here, as in other cases of the same kind, the story originated from the proverb, not the proverb from the story. The story was told to explain the existence of the proverb, but the existence of the proverb itself is the ultimate fact. It happens to be a fact of historical significance. We may infer that the Christian tonsure had been introduced and enforced by Patrick, but that his rule was relaxed and disregarded after his death, the native clergy adopting the old native tonsure of the Druids. The two fashions subsisted for a time side by side, then the Roman fell completely out of use till it was restored in the seventh century. But the proverb "Mael is like unto Caplait" arose when the two tonsures were in use together, and expressed the claim that the native mode was as legitimate for a monk as the foreign.

From Rathcrochan, Patrick and his company proceeded westward and planted religious foundations in the region which is now most easily described as the barony of Castlereagh. A number of Gallic clergy were with him, and these he dispersed to found churches in various places. One of these places stands out in interest, though it is of small account now. Baslic survives as the name of a parish, and preserves the memory of the foreign clerks who thought of the greater *basilicae* of the Empire when they built their little sanctuary in the wilds of Connaught and gave it the high-sounding name of *Basilica sanctorum*. No place-name, due to Christianity, in Ireland has a greater interest than Basilica, west of Rathcrochan. Another church founded in this region, near the banks of the river Suck, was Cell Garad, which is perhaps to be sought at Oran, where an old burial-ground and the fragment of a belfry mark an ancient ecclesiastical site. Both Baslic and Cell Garad were the seats of bishops.

Patrick then went northward to Selce,[15] in the land of Brian. Here the sons of Brian welcomed him and were baptized, and he founded a church close to Lake Selce. On a hill hard by, where he and his companions encamped, a memorial of their visit was preserved for centuries. They wrote upon some stones in the place, and it was probably their own names that they recorded, so that posterity knew who were of Patrick's company when the sons of Brian were baptized at the hill of Selce. Two bishops were with him, Bron, whose home, as we saw, was in the north, on the seashore under Knocknaree, and Sachall, bishop of the new church of Baslic; eight priests, including Benignus, his favourite pupil; and two women. It may have been that the names of the company were inscribed on three stones severally consecrated by the names *Iesus, Christus, Soter*.

From here Patrick may have proceeded westward to Lake Tecet—Lake Tecet of Ireland, bearing the same name as the more famous Lake Tecet of Britain, which the stranger knows as the Lake of Bala. The boggy soil makes the waters dark, and if we look down from one of the hills which partly gird it, the form of the lake, with its many corners and inlets, eludes the eye. It was probably near the western or northern shore that Adrochta, who took the veil from Patrick's hand, founded a church. Nor is she forgotten to-day, for as we walk on the eastern bank of the lake, we are in the parish of "Adrochta's Church."[16]

We now come to a journey of Patrick for which we have a definite chronological indication, since we know that it was undertaken soon after the death of king Amolngaid, and that king probably died about thirteen years after Patrick's arrival in Ireland. The story represents the land of Amolngaid as the particular region of Fochlad which had been the goal of Patrick's desires, and describes the occasion of his setting forth as if it had been brought about by a pure chance. Near the palace of king Loigaire at Tara he overheard a conversation between two noblemen, one of whom informed the other that he was Endae, son of Amolngaid, and had come from the far west, "from Mag Domnon[17] and the wood of Fochlad." Then Patrick, hearing the magic name of his dream, was thrilled with joy, and, turning round, he cried to Endae, "Thither I will go with thee, if I live, for God bade me go." But Endae replied, "Thou shalt not come with me, lest we be slain together." "Yet," said the saint, "thou shalt never reach thy home alive if I come not with thee, nor shalt thou have eternal life. For it is on my account that thou hast come hither." And Endae said, "Baptize my son, for he is young. But I and my brethren may not believe in thee till we come to our own folk, lest they mock us." And Patrick baptized his son Conall.

It appears that Endae and his six brethren had come to Tara to invoke the judgment of the High King in a dispute about the inheritance of their father's property. The claim of Endae and his son was opposed to the claims of the other six. In giving judgment king Loigaire is said to have invited the aid of Patrick, and they decided that the inheritance should be divided among the claimants in seven parts. This doom was in favour of Endae's brethren, if, as we may suppose, Endae's claim was that the division of the property should be eightfold, his son Conall receiving a separate portion for himself. But however this may have been, Endae is said to have dedicated his seventh portion and his son Conall to Patrick and Patrick's God.

When the award was given, Patrick and a company of ecclesiastics prepared to set forth with Endae. But they took the precaution of making a formal agreement with Endae and his brothers, and we may be certain that whatever the other terms may have been, the bodily safety of the Christians was expressly ensured. The most significant circumstance concerning this treaty is that it was made under the warranty of king Loigaire. This is an important piece of evidence as to the attitude of that king to the Christian teachers. It exhibits his policy of enlightened toleration, and shows that, though personally he clung to the beliefs of his fathers, yet in his capacity of king of Ireland he was willing to assist the diffusion of a doctrine subversive of those beliefs.

Patrick set out with Endae and his brethren, and having crossed the river Moy, perhaps at a ford where the "town of the ford" stands to-day,[18] they entered the territory of Amolngaid, where were the woods of Fochlad, and beyond, to westward, the wild Mag Domnon. That the baptism of Conall and the coming of the Christian teacher in the company of the chiefs should arouse wrath and disgust among the Druids is not surprising, and there may be some historical foundation for the legend which tells how the chief Druid, Rechrad, sought to kill Patrick. Along with nine Druids, arrayed in white, he advanced to meet Endae and his company. When Endae saw them, he snatched up his arms to drive them off, but Patrick raised his left hand and cursed the wizard, and Rechrad fell dead, and was burned up before the eyes of all. The other Druids fled into Mag Domnon. And when the folk saw this miracle, many were baptized on that day.

It was in this way, according to the legend, that Christianity entered the northern regions of Fochlad. Near the forest, and close to the seashore, was founded a church,[19] and not far from it a cross was set up, of which the memory is preserved in the local name Crosspatrick.[20] The church, built doubtless of timber, was afterwards to be overshadowed by the neighbouring foundation of Killala, conspicuous by its lofty belfry. Elsewhere Patrick caused a square church of earth to be constructed, at the gathering-place of the sons of Amolngaid, which has been identified with Mullaghfarry, "the hill of the meeting-place."

VIII

FOUNDATION OF ARMAGH
AND ECCLESIASTICAL ORGANISATION

§1. *Visit to Rome* (*circa* A.D. 441–3)

IT is possible that Patrick had intended in earlier years to visit Rome long before he began his labours in Ireland. If he entertained such a thought, it would seem that circumstances hindered him from realising it. But it would not have been unnatural if he continued to cherish the idea of repairing to the centre of western Christendom; and we might expect that when he had spent some years in the toils, afflictions, and disappointments, the alternating hopes and fears, the successes and defeats, incident to missionary work in a barbarous land, he would have wished to receive some recognition of his work and sympathy with his efforts from the head of the western churches. He might count upon sympathy and encouragement; the interest which the Roman see was prepared to take in the remote island had been shown by the sending of Palladius; whether Patrick had ever himself received a message from the successor of Celestine is unknown.

In addition to the object of directing the attention of the Roman bishop to the growth of the Church in Ireland—an object which would at that time appeal strongly to Patrick or to any one else in his place—there was another motive for visiting Rome, which, though subordinate, must not be passed over. Patrick was the son of his age, and it would display a complete ignorance of the spirit of the Church, in Gaul and elsewhere at that time, if we failed to recognise the high importance which he must have attributed to the relics of holy men, especially of the early apostles, and the value which he would have set on acquiring such parcels of matter for his new churches in Ireland. The religious estimation of relics had become general in the fourth century. Such a learned man as Gregory of Nyssa set great store by them. The subject might be illustrated at great length, but it will be enough to remind the reader of the excitement which was caused in the religious world in the year 386 A.D., when Ambrose of Milan discovered the tombs of St. Gervasius and St. Protasius. The bishops of the west vied for shares in the remains. In Gaul, three cities, Tours, Rouen, and Vienne, were fortunate enough to receive scraps of linen or particles of blood-stained dust which had touched the precious bodies. The estimation of relics in Gaul will be best understood by reading the work of Victricius, Bishop of Rouen and missionary of Belgica, "in praise of the saints."[1] It is certain that Patrick could not have helped sharing in this universal reverence for relics, and could not have failed to deem it an object of high importance to secure things of such value for his church. The hope of winning a fragment of a cerement cloth or some grains of dust—*pulvisculum nescio quod in modico vasculo pretioso linteamine circumdatum*[2]— would have been no small inducement to visit Rome, the city of many martyrs.

Patrick had been eight years in Ireland when a greater than Celestine or Xystus was elected to the see of Rome.[3] The pontificate of Leo the Great I marks an eminent station in the progress of the Roman bishops to that commanding position which they were ultimately to occupy in Europe. His path had been prepared by his forerunners, but it is he who induces the Emperor to accord a formal and imperial sanction to the sovran authority of the Roman see in the west,[4] and he plays a more leading and decisive part than any of his predecessors in moulding Christian theology by his famous Epistle on the occasion of the Council of Chalcedon. That Leo should have taken as direct and energetic an interest in the extension of the borders of Christendom as the less eminent bishops before him is what we should expect.

It was in the year after his elevation that Patrick, according to the conclusion to which our evidence points, betook himself to Rome. No step could have been more natural, and none could have been more politic. It was equally wise whether he was assured of the goodwill of Leo or, as is possible, had reason to believe that his work had been misrepresented. To report the success of his labours to the head of the western churches, of which Ireland was the youngest, to enlist his personal sympathy, to gain his formal approbation, his moral support, and his advice, were objects which would well repay a visit to Rome, and an absence of some length from Ireland. It is indeed hardly too much to say that nothing was more likely to further his success than an express approbation of his work by the highest authority in Christendom.

But it is possible that he may have had a more particular motive, which may explain why he chose just this time for his visit. Hitherto, active in different parts of the island, he had established no central seat, no primatial or "metropolitan" church for the chief bishop. Not long after his return, he founded, as we shall see presently, the church of Armagh, fixing his own see there, and establishing it as the primatial church. This was a step of the highest importance in the progress of ecclesiastical organisation, and it is not a very daring conjecture to suppose that Patrick may have wished to consult the Roman bishop concerning this design and obtain his approbation.

The result of the visit to Rome is briefly stated in words which are probably a contemporary record, "he was approved in the Catholic faith." He may well have received practical advice from Leo—such advice as a later pontiff gave to Augustine for the conversion of the English. But Patrick bore back with him to Ireland visible and material proofs of the goodwill of Rome. He received gifts which, to Christians of his day, seemed the most precious of all gifts, relics not of any lesser martyrs, but of the apostles Peter and Paul. They were gifts particularly opportune for bestowing prestige upon the new church which he was about to found, and where they were afterwards preserved.

§2. *Foundation of Armagh* (A.D. 444)

No act of Patrick had more decisive consequences for the ecclesiastical history of the island than the foundation, soon after his return from Rome, of the church and monastery of Ardd Mache, in the kingdom of Oriel. King Daire, through whose goodwill this community was established, dwelled in the neighbourhood of the ancient fortress of Emain, which his own ancestors had destroyed a hundred years agone, when they had come from the south to wrest the land from the Ulidians and sack the palace of its lords. The conquerors did not set up their own abode in the stronghold of the old kings of Ulster; they burned the timber buildings and left the place desolate, as it were under a curse. The ample earth structures of this royal stronghold are still there, attesting that Emain, famous in legend, was a place of historical importance in the days when Ulster belonged to one of the elder peoples of the island.[5] Once and again, long after the days of St Patrick, the Picts from their home in Dalaradia made vain attempts to recover their storied palace, but it was not destined to become a place of human habitation again until, more than a thousand years after its desolation, a house seems to have been built there by an Ulster king "for the entertainment of the learned men of Ireland."

The abode of king Daire was somewhere in the neighbourhood. It seems possible that he was the king of Oriel, though it may be held that he was only king of one of the tribes which belonged to the Oriel kingdom. Daire was not ill disposed towards the foreign religion, and he was persuaded to grant Patrick a site for a monastic foundation not far from his own dwelling. Eastward from Emain, concealed from the eye by two high ridges, rises the hill known as Ardd Mache, "the height of Macha," bearing the name, it is said, of some heroine of legend. At the eastern foot of this hill, Daire apportioned a small tract of ground to Patrick, and this was the beginning of what was to become the chief ecclesiastical city of Ireland. The simple houses which were needed for a small society of monks were built, and there is a record, which appears to be ancient and credible, concerning these primitive buildings. A circular space was marked out, one hundred and forty feet in diameter, and enclosed by a rampart of earth. Within this *less,* as it was called, were erected, doubtless of wood, a Great House to be the dwelling of the monks, a kitchen, and a small oratory.[6] This record has an interest beyond this particular monastery, as we may believe that it represents the typical scheme of the monastic establishments of Patrick and his companions.

We know not how long Patrick and his household abode under the hill of Macha, but this settlement was not to be final.[7] It seems that the bishop ultimately won great influence over the king, who evidently embraced the Christian faith; and then Daire resolved that the monastery should be raised from its lowly place to a loftier and safer site. A curious story, with the marks of antiquity about it, has come down, showing how all this befell, and it would be difficult to say how much is fable and what was the underlying fact. Patrick, so the tale relates, had from the very first cast his eyes upon the hill of Macha. But Daire refused to grant it, and gave him instead the land below. One day a squire of the king drove a horse to feed in a field of grass which belonged to the monastery. Patrick remonstrated, but the squire made no answer, and when he returned to the field on the morrow, he found the horse dead. He told his master that the Christian had killed the horse, and Daire said to his men, Go and kill him. But as the men were on their way to do his bidding, an illness unto death suddenly fell on Daire, and his wife said, "It is the sake of the Christian. Let some one go quickly, and let his blessing be brought to us, and thou shalt be well; and let those who went to slay him be stopped." Then two men went to Patrick and told him that Daire was ill, and asked him for a remedy. Patrick gave him some water which he had consecrated. With this water they first sprinkled the dead horse, and it was restored to life; and then, returning to Daire's house, they found it no less potent in restoring their lord to health.

Then Daire visited the monastery to pay respect to Patrick, and offered him a large bronze vessel, imported from over seas. The bishop acknowledged the gift by a simple "I thank thee," in Latin. The king looked for some more elaborate and impressive acknowledgment; he was annoyed that the cauldron should be received with no greater sign of satisfaction than a *gratzacham,* as the Latin phrase *gratias agamus* sounded in rapid colloquial pronunciation. And on returning home he sent his servants to bring back the bronze, as a thing which the Christian was unable to appreciate. When they came back with the vessel, Daire asked them what Patrick said, and they replied, "He said *gratzacham.*" "What," said Daire, "*gratzacham* when it was given, *gratzacham* when it was taken away! It is a good word, and for his *gratzacham* he shall have his cauldron." Then Daire went himself with the cauldron to Patrick, and said, "Keep thy cauldron, for thou art a steadfast and unchangeful man." And he gave him, besides, the land which he had before desired.

Whatever may be thought of the anecdotes of the horse and the cauldron, we may believe that Patrick won the respect of Daire as a man of firm character, and that for this reason Daire was induced to promote him to the higher site, granting him the land on the hill, with the usual reservation of the rights of the tribe.[8] So it came about that Patrick and his household went up from their home at the foot of the hill and made another home on its summit. The new settlement was probably constructed on the same plan, though the close may have been larger, to suit the area of the hill-top. The old settlement below was perhaps devoted to the uses of a graveyard, and in later days a cloister was to arise there, known as the Temple of the Graveyard.

Such, according to ancient tradition, was the founding of Armagh, which rose to be the supreme ecclesiastical city in Ireland. Though we have no record of Patrick's own views, it is hardly possible to escape the conclusion that he consciously and deliberately laid the foundations of this preeminence. It is true that some of his successors in the see supported and enhanced its claim to supremacy and domination by misrepresentations and forgeries, just as in a larger sphere the later bishops of Rome made use of fabricated documents and accepted falsifications of history in order to establish their extravagant pretensions. But as in the case of Rome, so in the case of Armagh, misrepresentation of history could only avail to increase or confirm an authority which was already acknowledged and to extend the limits of a power which had been otherwise established. If the church of Armagh had been originally on the same footing as any of the other churches which were founded by Patrick, it is inconceivable that it could have acquired the pre-eminence which it enjoyed in the seventh century merely by means of the false assertion that the founder had made it supreme over all his other churches. Now we know of no political circumstances or historical events between the age of Patrick and the seventh century which would have served to elevate the church of Armagh above the churches of northern Ireland and invest it with an authority and prestige which did not originally belong to it. The only tenable explanation of the commanding position which Armagh occupied is that the tradition is substantially true, and that Patrick made this foundation, near the derelict palace of the ancient Ulster kings, his own special seat and residence, from which he exercised, and intended that his successors should exercise, in Ireland an authority similar to that which a metropolitan bishop exercised in his province on the continent.[9] The choice of Armagh may seem strange. It may be said that if his "province" was conterminous with the whole island, the hill of Macha was hardly a well-chosen spot as an ecclesiastical centre. We might expect him to have sought a site somewhere in the kingdom of Meath, somewhere less distant from the hill of Uisnech, which the islanders regarded as the navel of their country. Trim, for instance, would seem to be a far more suitable seat for a bishop whose duties of supervision extended to Desmond as much as to Dalriada. There are two points here which may be taken into consideration. If we confine our view to the sphere of Patrick's own missionary activity, namely, northern Ireland, Armagh was a sufficiently convenient centre. Meath and Connaught and the kingdoms of Ulster, the lands in which Patrick had himself chiefly worked, might seem to require closer supervision, and it may have been a matter of policy not to attempt to press his authority too strictly over the churches of the south. We shall see presently that though he visited southern

Ireland, his work there was relatively slight. The evidence suggests that while the whole island formed a single ecclesiastical province, in which Patrick occupied the position of "metropolitan," there was actually, though not officially, a province within a province. He exerted a more direct and minute control over the northern part of the island. But, in any case, the position of an ecclesiastical metropolis cannot be entirely determined by compasses; geographical convenience cannot be always decisive. Here we come to a second consideration. The circumstance that king Loigaire was not a Christian may have weighed with Patrick against choosing a place in Meath. He may have thought it expedient to fix the chief seat of ecclesiastical authority in the territory and near the palace of a Christian king. If Daire was king of Oriel, his conversion to Christianity, in contrast with the obduracy of Loigaire, will go far to explain the choice of Armagh. It counted for much to have a secure position near the gates of a powerful king, and his conversion would have been the greatest single triumph that Patrick had yet achieved.

Our oldest records do not describe Patrick's work in the kingdoms of Ulster with the same details or at the same length as his work in Connaught. But they indicate that he preached and founded churches in the kingdoms of Ailech and Oriel, as well as in Ulidia; and there is reason to believe that fuller records existed at an early period and were used by one of the later biographers. It may be noted that he is said to have consecrated the site of a church at Coleraine, and that a stone on which he sat was shown at Dunseveric, on the shore of the northern sea. In the land of the Condiri, who gave their name to the diocese of Connor, many churches attributed their origin to him, for instance, Glenavy,[10] near the banks of Lake Neagh, and Glore, the church of Glenarm.

§3. *In South Ireland*

While Patrick's sphere of immediate activity seems to have been mainly the northern half of the island, there is not much room for serious doubts that he claimed to hold a position of ecclesiastical authority over the southern provinces also. His own description of himself not as bishop in a particular province, but as bishop in Ireland generally,[11] is sufficient to make this clear; and there are not wanting ancient records of his visits to Leinster and Munster. He is said to have baptized the sons of Dunlang, king of Leinster, and Crimthann, king of the Hy Ceinselaich; he is recorded to have visited the royal palace at the hill of Cashel and baptized the sons of Natfraich, king of Munster. It was remembered that he had passed through Ossory, and worked in the regions of Muskerry. If, as is possible, Christianity had made greater way in the southern kingdoms, he had less to do as a pioneer, but the task of organisation must have devolved upon him here as in the north. It is easy to understand why comparatively scanty traditions should have been preserved of his work in the south. His special association with the see of Armagh did not dispose the communities of Munster and Leinster to remember a connexion which supported the claims of that see to a superior jurisdiction.

In Leinster, Patrick had two fellow-workers who occupied a special position. Auxilius and Iserninus, whom he had known at Auxerre, had been sent to Ireland about six years after his own coming.[12] The origin of Auxilius is unknown. His name is still commemorated by a church which he founded, Kill-ossy,[13] not far from Naas, one of the chief abodes of the kings of Leinster. Iserninus was of Irish birth. His native name was Fith. He was born in the neighbourhood of Clonmore, on the borders of Carlow and Wicklow. Here, in the land of his clan, he first set up a church, but his ultimate establishment was at Aghade,[14] on the Slaney. These regions formed part of a considerable kingdom which was at this time ruled over by Endae Cennsalach, who seems to have founded the political importance of his tribe, for the land came to be known by the name of the Children of Cennsalach. This king did what lay in his power to oppose the diffusion of the new faith, and Iserninus found it prudent to withdraw beyond the borders of his kingdom. Perhaps he found a refuge at Kil-cullen,[15] close to Dún Aillinn, one of the strongholds of the kings of Leinster. But Crimthann, the son and successor of Endae, was converted and baptized by Patrick at his dwelling in Rathvilly, on the banks of the Slaney, where earthworks still mark a seat of the kings of the Children of Cennsalach. This case is similar to the case of the sons of Amolngaid, and illustrates the general fact that while the older generation was still, fervently or patiently, clinging to the old beliefs, the younger generation was steadily turning to the new. The conversion of Crimthann enabled Iserninus to return to his own land, and he established himself at Aghade, a crossing-place on the Slaney, about nine miles below Rathvilly.

Among the acts which are ascribed to Patrick in Le-inster, the consecration of Fíacc, the Fair, a pupil of the poet Dubthach, and himself a poet, deserve mention. The conversion of the poet into the Christian bishop reminds us of the more illustrious contemporary case of Sidonius Apollinaris. There seems no reason to doubt the truth of this tradition, and perhaps the bell, the staff, the writing tablet, and the cup and paten, which Patrick is said to have given to Fíacc, were preserved at the church where his memory was specially cherished. He was first settled at a church which was called after himself, Domnach Féicc, the situation of which is not improbably supposed to have been east of the Slaney, not far from Tallow. But he afterwards became bishop of Slébte, on the western bank of the Barrow, under the hills of Margy,[16] and ended his days there. In the early middle ages Slébte was a notable place on the ecclesiastical map, but the desolate site shows no vestiges of its ancient importance. At the end of the seventh century Slébte renewed the ties which bound it to Armagh in the days of Fíacc and Patrick, and we possess a monument of this reconciliation in the earliest biography of Patrick that has come down to us, written by a clerk of Fíacc's church.

§4. *Church Discipline*

It is not clear whether Auxilius and Iserninus were already invested with episcopal rank when they left Gaul, or were consecrated in Leinster by Patrick. But in any case, they seem, along with Secundinus, who came with them from Gaul, to have held an exceptional position of weight as counsellors and coadjutors. Coming, perhaps, from the episcopal city where Patrick himself had been trained, they corroborated the Gallic influence, we might say the influence of Auxerre, which presided at the organisation of the Church in Ireland. It was natural that Patrick should take special counsel with these men for laying down rules of ecclesiastical discipline, and, on the occasion, perhaps, of one of his visits to Leinster, a body of rules was drawn up in the form of a circular letter, addressed by Patrick, Auxilius, and Iserninus to all the clergy of Ireland.[17] The miscellaneous regulations are arranged in a haphazard manner, and were evidently prompted by abuses or practical difficulties which had come to the notice of the framers. Most of the rules deal with the discipline of the clergy. They testify to such irregularities as a bishop interfering in his neighbour's diocese; vagabond clerks going from place to place; churches founded without the permission of the bishop. It is ordained that no cleric from Britain shall minister in Ireland, unless he has brought a letter from his superior. All the clergy, from the priest to the doorkeeper, are to wear the complete Roman tonsure, and their wives are to veil their heads. A monk and a consecrated virgin are not to drive from house to house in the same car, or indulge in protracted conversations. Provision is made for the stringent enforcement of sentences of excommunication. One of the most important duties of Irish Christians at this period was the redemption of Christian captives from slavery;[18] and this furnished an opportunity for imposture and deception. It is provided that no one shall privately and without permission make a collection for this purpose, and that, if there be any surplus from a collection, it shall be placed on the altar and kept for another's need.

It is interesting to observe a prohibition of the acceptance of alms from pagans. It points to the comprehensive religious view of some, perhaps many, of the still unconverted—Loigaire himself may have been an instance,—who, though not prepared to abandon their own cults, were ready to pay some homage to the new deity whose reality and power they did not question.

In a church growing up in a heathen land, it seems to have been found inexpedient and impracticable to enforce long periods of penitence for transgressions which were regarded more lightly in Ireland than in the Roman Empire. Accordingly we find that only a year of penance is imposed on those who commit manslaughter or fornication or consult a soothsayer,[19] and only half a year for an act of theft.

The provisions contained in this circular letter cannot represent all the rules which Patrick, with his coadjutors, must have made for ecclesiastical order in Ireland. A number of other canons were ascribed to him, and though we cannot be sure that they are all authentic, it cannot be proved that they are all of later origin. One of them, not the least important, is a provision which, without any express evidence, we might surmise that Patrick would have ordained. It required no special discernment to foresee that in a young church difficult questions would inevitably arise which might lead to grave controversy and dissension. How were such to be decided? Could they safely be left to local councils, with no higher court of appeal? The obvious resource was to follow the common practice of other western churches and request the Bishop of Rome to lay down a ruling. For Patrick, as for his contemporaries, this was simply a matter of course. To consult the Roman see, and obtain a ruling in the form of a decretal, was the universally recognised means in the western provinces of securing unity and uniformity in the Church. The position which the Roman see occupied, by common consent, in the days of Patrick has been sufficiently explained in a previous chapter;[20] and if this position is rightly understood, it becomes evident that, when Ireland entered into the ecclesiastical confederation of the west, it was merely a direct and inevitable consequence that, for the church in Ireland, just as for the churches in Gaul or in Spain, the Roman see was both a court of appeal, and also the one authority to which recourse could be had, whenever recourse to an authority beyond Ireland itself seemed desirable. This was so axiomatic that, if we are told that Patrick expressly prescribed resort to Rome in case of necessity, the only thing which might surprise us is that he should have thought it needful to formulate it at all. But in a new church, unfamiliar with the traditions of the older churches within the Empire, it was clearly desirable to define and enact some things which were observed in Gaul and Spain and Italy without express definition or enactment. We are therefore fully entitled to accept as authentic the canon which lays down, "If any questions (of difficulty) arise in this island, let them be referred to the apostolic seat."[21] Not to have recognised the Roman see as the source of authoritative responses would have been almost equivalent to a repudiation of the unity of the Church.

That Patrick should have prescribed to Irish monks the form of tonsure which was usual in western monasteries was a matter of course. It was more significant that he introduced, as seems to be the case, the Paschal reckoning which was at that time approved by Rome. It would appear that an older system for the determination of Easter was in use among the

Christian communities which existed in Ireland before his coming. He brought with him a table of Easter days based on the system then accepted at Rome, so that in the celebration of this feast the new province might be in harmony with western Christendom.

Though we have no direct testimony as to the liturgy which Patrick introduced, we cannot doubt that it was the Gallican. The Gallican liturgy, which differs from the Roman by its oriental character, prevailed in Ireland and Britain up to the end of the seventh century; and we are entitled to conjecture, in the absence of evidence to the contrary, that Patrick, trained at Auxerre, introduced the usage to which he was accustomed in that church.

§5. *Ecclesiastical Organisation*

St Patrick has himself briefly described some of the features of his work, and his description bears out and supplements the general impression which we derive from the details recorded by tradition. In the first place, he indicates the double character of his work. On the one hand he created an ecclesiastical organisation, he chose and ordained clergy, for a people which had been recently turning to the Christian faith.[22] On the other hand, he planted that faith in regions which were wholly heathen, in the extreme parts of the island, as he repeatedly insists.[23] He spread his nets that a large multitude "might be caught for God," and that there might be clergy everywhere to baptize and exhort a folk needing and craving their service.[24] He says that he baptized thousands, and this need not be a figure of hyperbole,[25] and ordained

ministers of religion everywhere. The foundation of monastic communities is borne out by his incidental observation
that young natives have become monks, and daughters of
chieftains "virgins of Christ."[26] These maidens, he says, generally took their vows against the will of their fathers, and
were ready to suffer persecution from their parents. He mentions especially a beautiful woman of noble birth whom he
baptized. A few days after the ceremony she came to him and
intimated that she had received a direct warning from God
that she should become a "virgin of Christ." It is not suggested that the opposition of the parents was due to heathen
obduracy; it would rather appear that, in the cases which
are here contemplated, the parents themselves had likewise
embraced Christianity. But they had a natural repugnance
to seeing their children withdrawn from the claims of the
family and the world. The triumph on which Patrick in this
passage complacently dwells is not the triumph of Christian
doctrine but of the monastic ideal.

Patrick refers to perils through which he passed in the
prosecution of his work. He says that divine aid "delivered
me often from bondage and from twelve dangers by which
my life was endangered."[27] He mentions one occasion on
which he and his companions were seized, and his captors
wished to slay him. His belongings were taken from him and
he was kept in fetters for a fortnight, but then, through the
intervention of influential friends, he was set free and his
property restored.[28]

Such experiences would probably have been more frequent
if he had not resorted to a policy which stood him in good
stead. He used to purchase the goodwill and protection of the

kings by giving them presents.[29] In the same way he provided for the security of the clergy in those districts which he most frequently visited, by paying large sums to the judges or brehons. It is easily conceived that their goodwill was of high importance for harmonising the new communities and their new ideal of life with the general conditions of society. Patrick claims to have distributed among the judges at least "the value of fifteen men." All these expenses were defrayed from his own purse.[30]

Another feature in his policy, on which he prided himself, was plain dealing and sincerity towards the Irish. He never went back from his word, and never resorted to tricks, in order to win some advantage for "God and the Church." He believed that by adhering strictly to this policy of straightforwardness he averted persecutions.[31]

While Patrick was assisted by many foreign fellow-workers, it was his aim to create a native clergy; and it was a matter of the utmost importance to find likely youths and educate them for ecclesiastical work. Our records do not omit to illustrate this side of his policy. Benignus, who afterwards succeeded him in Armagh, was said to have been adopted by him as a young boy soon after his coming to Ireland,[32] and Sachall, who accompanied him to Rome, was another instance. A similar policy was contemplated by Pope Gregory the Great for England. We have a letter which he wrote to a presbyter, bidding him purchase in Gaul English boy slaves of seventeen or eighteen years, for the purpose of educating them in monasteries.[33]

The churches and cloisters which were founded by Patrick and his companions seem in most cases to have been established on land which was devoted to the purpose by chieftains or nobles from their own private property. But the interests of the tribe to which the proprietor belonged, and the interests of the proprietor's descendants, had to be considered, and the consideration of these interests seems to have led to a peculiar system. We find that in some cases the proprietor did not make over all his rights to the ecclesiastical community which was founded on his estate, but retained, and transmitted to his descendants, a certain control over it, side by side with the control which the abbot, a spiritual head of the community, exercised. There were thus two lines of succession—the secular line, in which the descent was hereditary, and the ecclesiastical line, which was sometimes regularly connected by blood with the founder. This dual system kept the ecclesiastical community in close touch with the tribe, and it has been pointed out that the tendency ultimately was "to throw the ecclesiastical succession into the hands of the lay succession, and so to defeat the object of the founder by transferring the endowment to the laity."[34] Armagh and Trim are conspicuous instances of this dual succession.

In other cases the connexion of the monastery with the tribe was secured, and the interests of the proprietor's family were consulted by establishing a family right of inheritance to the abbacy. There was only a spiritual succession; the undivided authority lay with the abbot; but the abbots could be chosen only from the founder's kin.[35] Such a provision might be made conditionally or unconditionally. It might be provided that preference should be given to members of the founder's family, if a person suitable for such a spiritual office

could be found among them. The monastery of Drumlease
in Leitrim, which was founded by one Fethfió, furnishes an
instructive example.[36] Fethfió laid down that the inheritance
to Drumlease should not be confined unconditionally to his
own family. His family should inherit the succession, if there
were any member pious and good and conscientious. If not,
the abbot should be chosen from the community or monks
of Drumlease.

But in other cases the original proprietor seems to have
alienated his land and placed it entirely in the hands of an
ecclesiastical founder, who was either a member of another
tribe or a foreigner. But the tribe within whose territory the
land lay had a word to say. It seems to have been a general
rule that the privilege of succession belonged to the founder's
tribe, but that if no suitable successor could be found in
that tribe, the abbacy should pass to the tribe within whose
territory the monastery stood.[37]

In our earliest records we find some ecclesiastical foundations expressly distinguished as "free," which would seem to
imply a release from restrictions and obligations which were
usually imposed, and a greater measure of independence of
the tribe.[38] Thus in Sligo a large district was offered by its
owners "to God and Patrick," and we are told that the king,
who seems to be acting as representative of the tribe, "made it
free to God and Patrick."[39] But it is impossible to determine
what were the limits of this immunity.

The Church in the Roman Empire has been described as
an *imperium in imperio,* and the typical ecclesiastical community in Ireland may be described as a tribe within a tribe.
The abbot, or, where the dual system prevailed, his lay

coadjutor, exercised over the lay folk settled on the lands
of the community a control similar to that which the tribal
king exercised over the tribe. But though the community
was thus constituted as an independent body and formed a
sort of tribe itself, not subject to the king, it was nevertheless
bound by certain obligations to the tribe within whose borders it lay. We have seen that the right of eventual succession
to the abbacy was often reserved to the tribe. But in general
the monastery was bound not only to furnish the religious
services which the tribe required, but to rear and educate
without cost the offspring of any tribesman who chose to
devote his son a religious life.[40] The tribesman, on his part,
was bound, when he had once consigned his child to the
care of the monks, not to withdraw him, on pain of paying
a forfeit.[41] A monastery might welcome novices from other
tribes, if their parents chose to pay the cost of their education; its attachment by a closer bond to what might be called
its lay tribe was expressed in this right of the tribesmen to a
free training for an ecclesiastical career.

It is also to be observed that the member of a religious
house, though he belonged to a society which managed its
affairs independently of the tribe, did not altogether cease
to be a tribesman.[42] If he was slain, the compensation was
due not to the church but to his tribe. It is uncertain how
far he continued to share any of the secular liabilities of his
lay tribesmen. On his father's death he inherited his portion of the family property, like any of his brethren; but
we cannot say how far, in early times, the tribe permitted
a monastic community to exercise rights over land thus inherited by one of its members. In later times the Church

assumed possession, perhaps allowing the monk to hold his inheritance as a tenant, and furnishing him with stock.[43] But this custom may not have been introduced until the Church had waxed in power and cupidity. It is uncertain, too, what claims the newborn monasteries ventured to press, in their early years, upon the liberality of those who had permitted their foundation. At a subsequent period they claimed[44] not only first-fruits and tithes and the firstlings of animals, but also first-born sons, and when a man had ten sons, another as well as the eldest. We may doubt whether such claims, modelled on the law of Moses, and exceeding in audacity the claims of any other church, were often admitted[45] or seriously pressed; but it is certain that rights of such a kind were not and could not have been sought by Patrick and his fellows.

This sketch of the conditions under which the new religious settlements were planted in Ireland is necessarily vague and slight, and is presented with the reserve which is due when the material for reconstruction is fragmentary and we have to argue back from circumstances which prevailed at a later period. But the evidence at least shows clearly that the organisation was conditioned and moulded by the nature of the secular society. On one hand there was a bond, of various degrees of intimacy, connecting the religious community with the tribe, in the midst of which it was established; and on the other hand, the community took upon itself the form and likeness of a tribe or clan, its members being regarded as the family or followers of its head.

There is no reason to suppose that all Patrick's ecclesiastical foundations took the shape of monastic societies. Many of the churches which he founded were served, doubtless, by only one or two clerics, and furnished with only enough land to support them. But the monastic foundations were a leading feature of the organisation. They were to be centres for propagating Christianity and schools for educating the clergy. But they also served the religious needs of the immediate district. A staff of clergy was attached, and the abbot was frequently also a bishop. It is not difficult to conjecture the reason and purpose of this remarkable union of the monastic institution with general church organisation. It was probably due to the circumstance that there were no cities in Ireland; centres had to be created for ecclesiastical purposes, and it was almost a matter of course that these ecclesiastical towns should be constructed on the monastic principle. If towns had existed, they would have been the ecclesiastical centres, the seats of the bishops; the bishops would not have been abbots or attached to monasteries. The fact that the word *civitas*, "city," was used to designate these double-sided communities illustrates the motive of this singular organisation.

But the peculiarity must not mislead us into the error of supposing that there was no diocesan organisation, or that the bishops whom Patrick ordained had not definite and distinct sees. It is inconceivable that in instituting bishops he should not have been guided by geographical considerations, or that in organising a clerical body he should not have submitted them to the jurisdiction of the bishops whom he ordained. The limits of the bishoprics would naturally have corresponded to the limits of tribal territories; this was not only the simplest scheme, but was also dictated by obvious political expedience. The anomalous state of things which presently arose, the multiplication of bishops without, sees, was assuredly never anticipated by Patrick. It was due to the extravagant growth of monasticism. When new monasteries were founded, they determined to have bishops of their own, and to be quite independent of the bishops of the dioceses in which they were situated. This practice was not indeed confined to Ireland. There are several notable instances in Gaul.[46] But whereas elsewhere it was the exception, in Ireland it seems to have become the rule. The desire of new foundations to be self-sufficient and completely independent of the diocesan bishop would not perhaps have been so strong if the diocesan bishop had not usually been associated with one of the older monasteries. But once the practice of bishops without sees was introduced, bishops multiplied like flies. A new and narrow conception of the episcopal office prevailed, and when it was recognised that bishops need not have sees, there was no reason to set a limit to their number. The order of bishop became a dignity to which any man of piety might aspire.

There is no evidence that Patrick consecrated bishops without sees, and perhaps it would not be rash to say that he never did so. It cannot be seriously doubted that he established a diocesan organisation, which, in the course of the subsequent development of religious institutions, largely broke down. The maintenance of the diocesan structure could not be secured without control from above, and unless we refuse to believe that Patrick attempted anything in the way of organisation, it is evident that he must have founded a superior archdiocesan or metropolitan jurisdiction. He exercised this higher authority himself, and it is difficult to doubt that he attached it to the see which he occupied, the see of Armagh. The position of this see has already engaged our attention. But the centrifugal tendencies which marked the secular society of Ireland made themselves felt no less acutely in the Church; the ecclesiastical communities were animated by the same impulse to independence as the tribes; and it was hard for the Bishop of Armagh, as for the King of Ireland, to exert effectual authority. The independent tribal spirit was not flexible or readily obedient to the distant control of a prelate who was a member of another tribe; there was no secular power able or willing to enforce submission to the higher jurisdiction. Thus it was a continual struggle for the bishops of Armagh to maintain the position which Patrick had bequeathed to them; and the rise within their province, during the sixth century, of new and powerful communities, owing them no obedience, and outstripping their church in zeal, learning, and reputation, conduced to the decline of their influence. It was not till the end of the seventh century that the church of Armagh began to succeed in re-establishing its power. In the meantime the interests of religion had perhaps not suffered through the absence of ecclesiastical unity. At no time were the churchmen of Ireland more conspicuous, and famous in other lands, for learning and piety than in the sixth and seventh centuries.

The difficulties and errors which have arisen as to the spirit and principles of Patrick's ecclesiastical policy are due to the circumstance that after his death his work was partly undone, and the Irish Church developed on lines which were quite from the purpose of his design. The old Easter reckoning survived his reform and lasted till the seventh century. Irish monks abandoned the recognised mode of shaving the head which he had enjoined, and adopted the native tonsure of the pagan Druids.[47] The central authority at Armagh could not maintain itself against the centrifugal spirit of the land or resist the love of local independence which operated in ecclesiastical exactly as in political affairs. Monasticism, an institution which appears to have been intensely attractive to the temper of the people, ran riot, we might say, at the expense of ecclesiastical organisation. Abbots became of more account than bishops. The political changes in Gaul and Italy, connected with the dismemberment of the Empire, tended to keep Ireland out of touch with the continental churches in the later part of the fifth and in the sixth century. The injunction to appeal to Rome, though no one would have thought of repudiating it, was a dead letter. Looking at Irish Christianity as it appears in the seventh century, when the movement set in to bring it into line with the rest of the western Church, students have been inclined to assume that Patrick inaugurated the peculiar features which were really alien to the spirit of his work. Whatever concessions and modifications he may have found it necessary or politic to make in view of the social conditions of Ireland, he certainly did not anticipate, far less intend, such a development as that which actually ensued.

But though his organisation partially collapsed, and though the Irish Christians did not live up to his ideal of the *unitas ecclesiae,* there was one feature of his policy which was never undone. He made Latin the ecclesiastical language of Ireland. The significance of this will claim our consideration when we come to examine his historical position. It was remembered in the traditions of his work that he used to write alphabets for youths who were chosen for a clerical career; it was the first step in teaching them Latin.

Some knowledge of the Latin alphabet must have penetrated to Ireland at an earlier period. It must have been known in the scattered Christian communities, and it may have been known much more widely. It was not a new thing when Patrick arrived, but his work seems to have secured it a new position. Yet we cannot say exactly what happened. We cannot say whether the introduction of the Latin script originated a written Irish literature, or only displaced an older form of writing in which a literature already existed. In the mist which rests over the early history of Ireland this is one of the darkest points. It would be out of place to discuss the question here at large, but one or two considerations may be briefly noted. The mode of writing which the early Irish possessed—though how long before the fifth century we know not—and seem to have mainly used for engraving names on sepulchral monuments, is alphabetic. The characters, which are called ogams, consisting of strokes and points, were probably a native invention, since such inscriptions are found only in Ireland and in regions of the British islands which came within the range of Irish influence. But it will not be maintained that the alphabet itself was a native product, an independent discovery. It is simply the Latin alphabet,[48] with the last three letters left out and two letters added.[49] And a cipher representing the Latin alphabet can hardly fail to imply that when it was invented the Latin alphabet was in use. No positive evidence has yet been discovered to show that the Irish ever employed, besides their monumental script, a less cumbersome system of symbols, suitable for literature and the business of life, other than the Roman. A few statements which may be gathered from their own later traditions are not sufficiently clear or authentic to carry much weight. The absence of evidence, however, is not decisive. It is to be remembered that writing was in use among the Celtic Iberians of Spain and the Celts of Gaul before the Roman Conquest. The Iberians had their own script, and some of the Spanish peoples had a considerable literature.[50] In Gaul, we are told by Caesar, the lore of the Druids was not written down, but Greek writing was used for public and private purposes.[51] This means that the Gallic tongue was written in Greek characters, and some examples of such writing are preserved.[52] These facts show at least that the art of writing might have reached Ireland at an early period. But there is no proof that it did. If any pre-Roman alphabet was ever used it has left no traces of its presence. But the Roman alphabet was introduced, perhaps much sooner than is generally supposed, after the Roman occupation of Britain. And from it some learned man in Ireland constructed the ogam cipher for sepulchral uses. The diffusion of Christianity tended, doubtless, to diffuse the use of writing, but Latin letters were a gift which the pagans of Ireland received from the Empire, independently of the gift of Christianity.

IX

WRITINGS OF PATRICK, AND HIS DEATH

§1. *The Denunciation of Coroticus*

CHRISTIANITY had been introduced among the Picts of Galloway at the beginning of the fifth century by the labours of a Briton, who is little more than a name. Ninian, educated at Rome, had probably come under the influence of St. Martin of Tours, and had then devoted himself to the task of preaching his faith in the wilds of Galloway, where, on the inner promontory which runs out towards the Isle of Man, he built a stone church. As the only stone building in this uncivilised land it became known as the White House (Candida Casa), and its place is marked by Whitern. An important monastic establishment grew around it, which enjoyed a high reputation in Ireland in the sixth century, and was known there as the "Great Monastery." The work of Ninian was, in one way, like the work of his contemporary Victricius in Gaul, being missionary work within the Roman Empire, if Galloway and its inhabitants belonged to the Roman province of Valentia. The Roman power may the more easily have controlled these barbarous subjects since they were severed from their kinsmen, the Picts of the north beyond the Clyde, by the British population of Strathclyde.

After the Roman legions were withdrawn from Britain, and the island was cut off from the central control of the Empire, the task of maintaining order in the western part of the "province of Valentia" seems to have been undertaken by one of those rulers who sprang up in various parts of the island, and are variously styled as "kings" or "tyrants." A word must be said as to the condition of Britain in the fifth century, because it is very generally misunderstood.

There can be no greater error than to suppose that the withdrawal of the Roman legions from Britain in 407, and the rescript of the Emperor Honorius, three or four years later, permitting the citizens of Britain to arm themselves and provide for their own defence, meant the instant departure of all things Roman from British shores, the death of Roman traditions, the end of Roman civilisation. The idea that the island almost immediately relapsed into something resembling its pre-Roman condition is due partly to the scanty nature of our evidence, partly to a misreading of the famous work of Gildas "on the decline and fall of Britain," partly to a mistaken idea of the isolation of Britain from the continent, and largely to that anachronistic habit, into which it is so easy to fall, of judging men's acts and thoughts as if they could have foreseen the future. It cannot be too strongly enforced that in those years which mark *for us* the Roman surrender of Britain, and for many years after, no man—emperor or imperial minister or British provincial—could have thought or realised that the events which they were witnessing meant a final dismemberment of the Empire in the west, that Britain was really cut off for ever. The Empire had weathered storms before, and emerged stable and strong; to the contemporaries of Honorius and Valentinian the Empire was part of the established order of things, and a suspension of its control in any particular portion of its dominion was something temporary and passing. The British provincials did not and could not for a moment regard themselves and their province as finally severed from Rome; they still considered themselves part of the Empire; for a hundred and fifty years some of them at least considered themselves Roman citizens. From this point of view alone it is not conceivable that the traditions and machinery of the Roman administration should have disappeared at once, the moment the central authorities ceased to control it. What could the provincials have deliberately put in its place? All the circumstances seem to enforce the conclusion that the administration, in its general lines, continued, but was gradually modified, and ultimately decayed, through three main causes—financial necessities which must have soon led to a reduction of the elaborate machinery of administration, the organisation of new methods of self-help, and the development of local interests promoted by the ambition of private persons who won power and supremacy in various districts. There was doubtless a Celtic revival, but for many years after the rescript of Honorius, Roman institutions must have continued to exist alongside of, or controlled by, the local potentates, who are described as "kings" or "tyrants." And in the later years of the fifth century the great successes won by the British against the English invaders were achieved by generals—Ambrosius Aurelianus, and Arthur—who were not "kings" or "tyrants," but rather, in some sense, national leaders, and whose position can be best explained by supposing that they represent the traditions of Roman rule, and are, in fact, successors of the Roman dukes and counts of Britain. If in some cases the tyrants may have combined their own irregular position with the title of a Roman official it is what we should expect.

The man whom we find in the reign of Valen-tinian III. ruling in Strathclyde, and maintaining such law and order as might be maintained, was named Coroticus or Ceretic, and he founded a line of kings who were still reigning at the end of the, following century. His seat was the Rock of Clyde.[1] As the seat of a British ruler, amid surrounding Scots and Picts, this stronghold came to be known as Dún na m-Bretan, "the fort of the Britons," which was corrupted into the modern Dumbarton. The continuity of the rule of Coroticus with the military organisation of the Empire is strongly suggested by the circumstance that his power was maintained by "soldiers";[2] and, his position seems thus marked as distinct from that of pre-Roman chiefs of British tribes. His soldiers may well be the successors of the Roman troops who defended the north. His position—whether he assumed any Roman military title or not—may be compared to that of the general Aegidius, who maintained the name of the Empire in north Gaul when it had been cut off from the rest of the Empire. Aegidius transmitted his authority to his son Syagrius, as Coroticus transmitted his to his son Cinuit; and if Syagrius had not been overthrown by the Franks, a state would have been formed in Belgica which would have resembled in origin the state which Coroticus formed in Strathclyde. Of course the Gallo-Roman generals Aegidius and Syagrius, while their authority was practically uncontrolled, were in touch with the Empire, maintained the Imperial machinery, and had a position totally different from the irregular position of the semi-barbarous Briton on his rock by the Clyde; but we may be sure that Coroticus was careful to make the most of his claim to represent the Imperial tradition and rule over Roman citizens. And while the contrast is obvious, it is not uninstructive to observe the analogy, which is less obvious, between the position of Britain and its rulers, still attached in theory, name, and tradition to the Empire, though cut off from it, and the position of those parts of the Belgic and Lyonnese provinces, which, aloof from the rest of Imperial territory, maintained themselves under Aegidius and his son Syagrius for a few years amid the surrounding German kingdoms.

Coroticus, then, was the ruler of Strathclyde in the days of Patrick. We can easily understand that he may sometimes have found it difficult to pay his soldiers and retainers, and that for this purpose he may have been forced to plunder his neighbours. However this may be, he fitted out a marauding expedition; it does not appear that he led it himself, but it crossed the channel, and descended on the coast of Ireland, probably in Dalaradia or Dalriada. Perhaps it was an act of reprisal for raids which the Scots and Picts of these lands may have made upon his dominion; it may have been, for all we know, an episode in a regular war. At all events he was supported in his enterprise by the Picts of Galloway, who had relapsed into heathenism, and by some of those heathen Scots who had come over from Ireland and settled in the region northwest of the Clyde. In the course of their devastation these heathen allies of Coroticus appeared on the scene of a

Christian ceremony. Neophytes, who had just been baptized and anointed with the baptismal chrism, were standing in white raiment; the sign of the cross was still "fragrant on their foreheads" when the heathen rushed upon them, put some to the sword and carried others captive. Patrick, whether he had himself performed the ceremony or not, must have been near the spot of this outrage, for he was informed of it so soon, that on the next day he despatched one of his most trusted priests—one whom he had trained from childhood —to the soldiers of Coroticus, requesting them to send back the booty and release the captives. The message, which must have reached them before they left Ireland, was received with mockery, though the soldiers of Coroticus were Christians and "Romans," and it was not they but their heathen allies who had massacred the defenceless Christians. It is not clear whether Coroticus himself was present when the message was delivered, but it is certain that Patrick regarded him as responsible, and we must suppose that he had declined to interfere before Patrick wrote the letter which is our record of this event. The only thing which the indignant bishop could do for the release of his "sons and daughters" was to bring the public opinion of the Christians in Strathclyde to bear upon Coroticus and his soldiers. He wrote a strong letter, addressing it apparently to the general Christian community in the dominion of Coroticus, and requiring them to have no dealings with the guilty "tyrant" and his soldiers, "not to take food or drink with them, not to receive alms from them, nor show respect to them, until they should repent in tears and make satisfaction to God by releasing the Christian captives." He asks that the letter should be read before all the people in the presence of Coroticus. The guilt of the outrage is laid, in this communication, entirely upon Coroticus; it is ascribed to his orders; he is called a betrayer of Christians into the hands of Scots and Picts. Apostrophising him the bishop writes: "It is the custom of Roman Christians in Gaul to send good men to the Franks and other heathens to redeem captives for so many thousand pieces of gold; you, on the contrary, slay Christians and sell them to a foreign nation that knows not God; you deliver members of Christ as it were into a house of ill fame."

The sequel of this episode is unknown. We have no record whether the letter of Patrick had any effect on the obstinate hearts of Coroticus and his soldiers, or whether those to whom it was addressed applied the pressure of excommunication, which he begged them to put in force. The Irish legend that the king was turned into a fox by the prayers of the saint is based on the idea that he declined to release the captives; but it may have no other foundation than the letter which we possess.

But this letter has an interest for the biographer of Patrick beyond the details of the occurrence which evoked it. Beside, and distinct from, the wrathful indignation which animates his language, there is a strain of bitterness which had another motive. He is clearly afraid that his message will not be received with friendship or sympathy by the British Christians to whom it is sent. He complains expressly that his work in Ireland is regarded in Britain—in his own country—with envy and un-charitableness. "If my own do not know me— well, 'a prophet has no honour in his own country.' We do not belong, peradventure, to one sheepfold, nor have we one

God for our father." He refers to his own biography, to his birth as a Roman citizen, to his unselfish motives in undertaking the toil of a preacher of the Gospel in a barbarous land where he lives a stranger and exile; as if he had to justify himself against the envy and injustice of jealous detractors. "I am envied"; "some despise me." This bitterness is a note of the letter, and almost suggests that in Patrick's opinion the envy and dislike with which his successful work in Ireland was regarded in north Britain was partly responsible for the outrage itself.

There is no extant evidence to fix the date of this episode, but the dominance of the same bitter note in the other extant writing of Patrick, which was written in the author's old age, makes it not improbable that the letter belongs to the later rather than to the earlier period of his labours in Ireland. To that other document, the *Confession,* we may now pass.

§2. *The Confession*

Men of action who help to change the face of the world by impressing upon it ideas which others have originated, have seldom the time, and seldom, unless they have received in their youth a literary training, the inclination, to record their work in writing. The great apostles of Europe illustrate this fact. None of them, from Wulfilas to Otto of Bamberg, has left a relation of his own apostolic labours. We are lucky if a disciple took thought for posterity by writing a brief narrative of his master's acts. But in the case of the apostle of the Scots, as in the case of the apostles of the Slavs, no disciple wrote down what he could aver of his own certain knowledge.

If Benignus, his pupil and successor, had done for Patrick what Auxentius did for Wulfilas, what Willibald did for Boniface, we should have certainty on many things where it is now only possible to note our ignorance. But although neither Patrick nor any of the other apostles who preached to Celt, German, or Slav wrote the story of his own life, some of them have left literary records which bear on their work. The most conspicuous example is the correspondence of our West-Saxon Boniface, the apostle of the Germans; but fortunately in Patrick's case, too, circumstances occasionally forced him to write. The *Confession* is of far greater interest and value than the letter against Coroticus; for, though not an autobiography, it contains highly important autobiographical passages, to which reference has been made in the foregoing pages.

This work was written in Patrick's old age, at a time when he felt that death might not be very far off. "This," he says, "is my confession before I die," and accordingly the work is known as the Confession. This title, however, might easily convey a false idea. The writer has occasion to confess certain sins, he has occasion also to make a brief confession of the articles of his faith, but it is in neither of these senses that he calls the work as a whole his Confession. Neither his sins nor his theological creed are his main theme, but the wonderful ways of God in dealing with his own life. "I must not hide the gift of God"; this is what he "confesses"; this is the refrain which pervades the *Confession* and emphatically marks its purpose.

Of miracles, in the sense of violations of natural laws, the *Confession* says nothing; but his own strange life seemed to Patrick more marvellous than any miracle in that special meaning of the word. The *Confession* reveals vividly his intense wondering consciousness of the fact that it had fallen just to him, out of the multitude of all his fellows who might have seemed fitter for the task, to carry out a great work for the extension of the borders of Christendom. As he looked back on his past life, it seemed unutterably strange that the careless boy in the British town should have shone forth as a light to the Gentiles, and the ways by which this strange thing had been compassed made it seem more mysterious still. But what impressed him above all as a divine miracle was that he should have felt assured of success beforehand. What we, in a matter-of-fact way, might describe as a man's overruling imperative desire, accompanied by a secret consciousness of his own capacity, to attempt a great and difficult task seemed to Patrick a direct revelation from one who had foreknowledge of the future—*qui novit omnia etiam ante tempora secularia.* The express motive of the *Confession* is to declare the wonderful dealings of God with himself, as a sort of repayment—*retributio*—or thanksgiving.[3]

But it would hardly have been necessary to make such a declaration in writing if it had not seemed to him that his life and work were partly misunderstood. It was inevitable that a man of Patrick's force of character and achievements should have aroused some feelings of jealousy and voices of detraction; and the *Confession* is evidently a reply to things that were said to belittle him. One charge that was brought against him was his lack of literary education. His deficiency in this respect was probably urged as a disqualification for the eminent position of authority which he had won by his practical labours. Compared with most of the many bishops in Gaul, compared perhaps with most of the few bishops in Britain, Patrick might well have been described as illiterate. In the eyes of his countryman, Faustus, in the eyes of Sidonius Apollinaris, the Bishop of Armagh would have seemed, so far as style is concerned, unworthy to hold a pen. On this count Patrick disarms criticism by a full admission of his *rusticitas,* his lack of culture, and acknowledges that as he grows old he feels his deficiency more and more. It was even this consciousness of literary incompetence that had hitherto withheld him from drawing up the *Confession* which he has at length resolved to write. Then he goes on to explain by passages from his life how it was that, though he missed the early training which is to be desired in a religious apostle, he had nevertheless presumed to take in hand the work of converting heathen lands. His narrative is designed to show that it was entirely God's doing, who singled him out, untrained and unskilled though he was; that there were no worldly inducements to support the divine command, which he obeyed simply without any ulterior motive, and in opposition to the wish of his kinsfolk. Here he is meeting another imputation, which stung him more than the true taunt of illiteracy. His detractors must have hinted that it was not with perfectly pure and unworldly motives that he had gone forth to preach among the Scots. He does not conceal that the island in which he had toiled as a captive slave had no attraction for him; he implies that he always felt there as a stranger in a strange land.[4] "I testify," he says, summing up, "in truth and in exultation of heart, before God and His holy angels, that I never had any motive save the gospel and promises of God, to return at any time to that people from which I had formerly escaped."[5] He repudiates especially the imputation that he won any personal profit in worldly goods from those whom he converted, or that he sought in any way to overreach the folk among whom he lived. To show how discreetly he ordered his ways, how careful he was to avoid all scandalous suspicion, he mentions that when men and women of his flock sent him gifts, or laid ornaments on the altar, he always restored them, at the risk of offending the givers.

It is easy enough to read between the lines the kind of detraction that wounded St Patrick; it may seem less easy to determine in what quarter the unfriendly voices were raised. But there are certain indications which enable us to suspect that it was in his own country and by his own countrymen that the charges to which he obliquely refers were brought against him. At the end of the composition he says that he wrote it "in Ireland"; and this gives us a reasonable ground for supposing that it was addressed mainly to people outside Ireland. When he speaks of "those peoples amidst whom I dwell," when he mentions "women of *our* race" (not "women of *my* race"), in contrast with women of Scottish birth,[6] we can hardly be wrong in thinking that he is addressing not his Irish disciples, but some of his British fellow-countrymen. And we may well believe that if this "apology" for his life had been meant in the first place for Ireland, he would have taken some care to veil his feeling of homelessness; he would not have shown so clearly that he felt as an alien on outlandish soil, and that he was abiding there only from a sense of duty, doing despite to the longings of his heart. This inference is borne out by the writer's express statement that he wishes his "brethren and kinsfolk" to know his character and nature.[7] Nor is it contradicted by the fact that he closely associates those whom he addresses with his own work.[8] On the contrary, this enables us to identify more precisely the origin of the detraction which evoked the *Confession*. The unfriends who disparaged him were clearly some of those British fellow-workers who had laboured with him in propagating the Christian faith in Ireland. That jealousy and friction should occur between the chief apostle and some of his helpers is only what we might expect, as in any similar case; and it may be that some of those who felt themselves aggrieved returned in disgust to Britain, and indulged their ill-will by spreading evil reports about Patrick's conduct of the Irish mission. It was for the communities in Britain where such reports were circulated, it was to refute those who set them afloat, that the *Confession* was in the first instance intended.

But Patrick had been exposed to one direct attack, which seems to have caused him more distress and agitation of spirit than any experience during his work in Ireland. Before he was ordained deacon, he had confessed to a trusted friend a fault which he had committed at the age of fifteen. His friend evidently did not consider it an obstacle to ordination, and subsequently supported the proposal that Patrick should be consecrated bishop for Ireland.[9] But afterwards he betrayed the secret, and the youthful indiscretion came to the ears of persons whom we may perhaps identify with some of Patrick's foreign coadjutors. "They came," he says in his rude style, "and urged my sins against my laborious episcopate." The words prove that he had already laboured for some years—other indications suggest fifteen or sixteen years—when this attack was made. He does not tell us how he met or weathered the danger; he ascribes his escape from stain and opprobrium to Divine assistance. We can sympathise with him in his deep resentment of an attack so manifestly unjust, of a friend's treachery apparently so inexcusable; but the incident clearly shows that there existed a party distinctly hostile to him, men who were ready to seize on any handle against him. His want of culture had been hitherto the chief reproach which they could fling; when they discovered a moral delinquency, though it was more than forty years old, the opportunity was irresistible.

But while the vindication was addressed to an audience beyond Ireland, it was intended also for the Irish. It might almost be described as an open letter to his brethren in Britain, published in Ireland. He describes it himself as "a bequest to my brethren, and to my children whom I baptized," for the purpose of making known "the gift of God," *donum Dei*.

The spirit and tone of this work are so consistently humble from first to last, that it almost lends itself to a misconstruction, in the sense that the measure of Patrick's achievements was smaller and the sphere of his work more restricted than our other sources give us to suppose. It has even been said that the *Confession* is a confession of a life's failure.[10] Any such interpretation misreads the document entirely. On the contrary, the main argument, as we have already seen, is that the success which Patrick had been led to hope and expect—through divine intimations as he believed—had been brought to pass. If success is not proved by vaunting, failure assuredly is not proved by the absence of boasts. But the proud consciousness of the writer that his life had been fruitful and prosperous comes out more subtly in the implied comparison which he suggests between himself and the first Apostle of the Gentiles, by quotations and echoes from Paul's epistles.[11]

It is pathetic to read how the exile would fain visit Britain, his home, and Gaul, where he had many friends, but feels himself bound by the spirit to spend the rest of his life (*residuum aetatis meae*) in his self-chosen banishment, to maintain his work, and especially to protect by his influence the Christians, whom dangers constantly threatened. His energy and undismayed perseverance had accomplished a great work, and he decided not to desert it till death compelled him.

His two writings furnish the only evidence we possess for forming an idea of his character. The other documents, on which we depend for the outline of his life and work, preserve genuine records of events, but reflect the picture of a man who must not be mistaken for the historical Patrick. The bishop, of British birth and Roman education, is gradually transformed into a typical Irish saint, dear to popular imagination, who curses men and even inanimate things which incur his displeasure. He arranges with the Deity that he shall be deputed to judge the Irish on the day of doom. The forcefulness of the real Patrick's nature is coarsened by degrees into caricature, until he becomes the dictator who coerces an angel into making a bargain with him on the Mount of Murrisk.[12] The stories of the Lives, so far as they characterise Patrick, present the conception, which the Irish formed of a hero saint. The accounts of his acts were not written from any historical interest, but simply for edification; and the monks, who dramatised both actual and, legendary incidents, were not concerned to regard, even if they had known, what manner of man he really was, but were guided by their knowledge of what popular taste demanded. The mediaeval hagiographer may be compared to the modern novelist; he provided literary recreation for the public, and he had to consider the public taste. In regard to the process by which Patrick was Hibernicised, or adapted to an Irish ideal, it is significant that the earliest literature relating to his life seems to have been written in Irish. This literature must have been current in the sixth century, and on it the earliest Latin records are largely based.

The writings of Patrick do not enable us to delineate his character, but they reveal unmistakably a strong personality and a spiritual nature. The man who wrote the *Confession* and the *Letter* had strength of will, energy in action, resolution without over-confidence, and the capacity for resisting pressure from without. It might be inferred, too, that he was affectionate and sensitive; subtle analysis might disclose other traits. But it is probable that few readers will escape the impression that he possessed besides enthusiasm the practical qualities most essential for carrying through the task which he undertook in the belief that he had been divinely inspired to fulfil it. A rueful consciousness of the deficiencies of his education weighed upon him throughout his career; we can feel this in his almost wearisome insistence upon his *rusticitas.* Nor has he exaggerated the defects of his culture; he writes in the style of an ill-educated man. His Latin is as "rustic" as the Greek of St. Mark and St. Matthew. He was a *homo unius libri*; but with that book, the Christian Scriptures, he was extraordinarily familiar. His writings are crowded with Scriptural sentences and phrases, most of them probably quoted from memory.

§3. *Patrick's Death and Burial* (A.D. 461)

It would appear that some years before his death Patrick resigned his position as head of the church of Armagh, and was succeeded by his disciple Benignus.[13] If this is so, it seems probable that he retired to Dalaradia, and spent the last three or four years of his life at Saul, in the Island-plain. Here he may possibly have written his *Confession*; here he certainly died. His death is encircled with legends which reflect the rival interests of Armagh and Downpatrick, but attest the fact that he died and was buried at the barn of Dichu. It was a disappointment to Armagh not to possess his body, and it was a stimulating motive for mythopoeic ingenuity to explain how this came to pass.

When the day of his death drew nigh, an angel came and warned him. Forthwith he made preparations, and started for Armagh, which he loved above all places. But as he went, a thorn-bush burst into flame on the wayside and was not consumed. And an angel spoke—not Victor, the angel who was accustomed to visit Patrick, but another sent by Victor—and turned him back, bidding him return to Saul, and granting him four petitions, as a consolation for the disappointment. Of these petitions two are significant. One was that the jurisdiction of his church should remain in

Armagh; the other that the posterity of Dichu should not die out. The first represents the interests of Armagh; the second clearly originated in the Island-plain.

Patrick obeyed the command of the angel, who also predicted that his death would "set a boundary against night." The rite of the Eucharist was administered to him at Saul by Bishop Tassach of Raholp, and at Saul he died[14] and was buried. After his death there was no night for twelve days, and folk said that for a whole year the nights were less dark than usually. And other wonders were recorded. Men told how angels kept watch over his body and diffused, as they travelled back to heaven, sweet odours as of wine and honey.

But miracles of this kind were not the only legends which gathered round the passing of the saint whom Armagh and Ulidia were alike eager to appropriate. The old strife between the kingdom of Ulidia and the kingdom of Orior[15] blazed up anew, in story, over Patrick's grave. The men of Orior advanced into the island-plain, and blood would have been shed on the southern banks of Lake Strangford if a Divine interposition had not stirred the waves of the bay, which by a sudden inundation dispersed the hosts and prevented a battle.[16] This was before the burial; but after the coveted body had been entombed, the men of Orior came again, resolved to snatch it from the grave.[17] Finding a waggon drawn by two oxen, they imagined the body was inside, and drove off, to discover, when they were near Armagh, that no body was there. They had been the victims of an illusion, designed, like the rising of the waters, to prevent the shedding of blood.

From these two myths an inference of a negative kind can be drawn with certainty. It is plain that, whatever controversy may have arisen concerning the burial of Patrick, there was no armed conflict. For the common motive of both legends is to account for the circumstance that the event did not lead to a war between the two peoples. But it would not be equally legitimate to draw the positive inference that the stories preserve the memory of a dispute, though not with arms, on the occasion of the saint's death. They point undoubtedly to a controversy and dispute, but this controversy and dispute may have arisen in subsequent years. The story of the angel's appearance reflects a conciliation between the claims of Saul and the claims of Armagh, and the two legends of the frustrated attempts of the men of Orior embody the same motive of peace and concord. Armagh had to acquiesce in the fact that Saul possessed Patrick's body; Saul acquiesced in the assertion that it was Patrick's own wish to lie at Armagh.

But this was not the only rivalry aroused by the desire of possessing the saint's mortal remains. When in later years a church was founded on the hill beside Dún Lethglasse, and overshadowed the older foundations of the neighbourhood, it was alleged that Patrick was buried in its precincts, and that the church was founded on that account. The story was invented that the angel gave him directions as to the fashion of his sepulture. "Let two untamed oxen be chosen, and left to go where they will." This was done. The oxen, drawing the body in a waggon, rested at Dún Lethglasse, and there it was buried.[18]

It is clear that all these tales must have taken shape at a considerable time after the saint's death. If his burial had actually caused any such commotion as the legends suppose, his tomb would assuredly have been conspicuous or well known, and no doubt could have arisen as to the place where he was laid. There would have been no room for the double claim of Saul and Dún Lethglasse. But so great was the uncertainty that it suggested a resemblance with Moses, whose grave was unknown. It is recorded, though it is not a record which we can implicitly trust, that St. Columba investigated and discovered the place of Patrick's sepulchre at Saul. These doubts and uncertainties justify us in concluding that Patrick was buried quietly in an unmarked grave, and that the pious excitement about his bones arose long after his death. And we can feel little hesitation in deciding that the obscure grave was at Saul. Of the three places which come into the story, Saul alone needs no mythical support for its claim, a claim in which Armagh itself acquiesces. Legend is called in to explain why the saint was not buried at Armagh; legend is called in to explain why he should be buried at Downpatrick; no legend is required to account for his burial at Saul.

No visible memorial of Patrick has escaped the chances of time, with one possible exception. In the Middle Ages the church of Armagh cherished with superstitious veneration two treasures which were believed to have belonged to him, a pastoral staff and a hand-bell. The crozier was deliberately destroyed in the war of sixteenth-century zealots against me-diaeval superstition, but the four-sided iron hand-bell still exists.[19] Both relics were very ancient, but to say that the bell was certainly Patrick's would be to go beyond our evidence, which only establishes a probability that it existed at Armagh a hundred years or so after his death.

X

PATRICK'S PLACE IN HISTORY

TWO extreme and opposite views have been held as to the scope and dimensions of St Patrick's work in Ireland. There is the old view that he first introduced the Christian religion and converted the whole island, and there is the view, propounded the other day, that the sphere of his activity was merely a small district in Leinster. The second opinion is refuted by a critical examination of the sources and by its own incapacity to explain the facts, while the first cannot be sustained because clear evidence exists that there were Christian communities in Ireland before Patrick arrived.

But the fact that foundations had been laid sporadically here and there does not deprive Patrick of his eminent significance. He did three things. He organised the Christianity which already existed; he converted kingdoms which were still pagan, especially in the west; and he brought Ireland into connexion with the Church of the Empire, and made it formally part of universal Christendom.

These three aspects of his work have been illustrated in the foregoing pages. His achievements as organiser of a church and as propagator of his faith made Christianity a living force in Ireland which could never be extinguished. Before him, it might have been in danger of extinction through

predominant paganism; after him, it became the religion of
Ireland, though paganism did not disappear. He did not introduce Christianity, but he secured its permanence, shaped
its course, and made it a power in the land.

Not less significant, though more easily overlooked, is the
rôle which he played by bringing Ireland into a new connexion with Rome and the Empire. Ordinary intercourse, as we
have seen, had been maintained for ages with Britain, Gaul,
and Spain; but now the island was brought into a more direct
and intimate association with western Europe by becoming
an organised part of the Christian world. There had been
constant contact before, but this was the first link.

The historical importance of this new bond, which marks
an epoch in the history of Ireland as a European country,
has been somewhat obscured through the circumstance that
after Patrick's death the Irish Church, though it did not sever
the link which he had forged, or dream of repudiating its incorporation as a part of Christendom, went a way of its own
and developed on eccentric lines. Relations with the centre were suspended, and this suspension seems to have been
due to two causes. The instinct of tribal independence, co-
operating with the powerful attraction which the Irish found
in monasticism, promoted individualism and disorganisa-
tion; monastic institutions tended to over-ride the episcopal
organisation founded by Patrick, and the resulting lack of
unity and general order was not favourable to the practical maintenance of that solidarity with Christendom which
was inaugurated by the sending of Palladius. But it was not
entirely due to the self-will and self-confidence of the Irish
themselves that they drifted from his moorings. The political

changes on the continent must also be taken into account. We can hardly doubt that but for the decline of the Imperial power and the dismemberment of the Empire in western Europe, the isolation[1] and eccentricity of the Irish Church in the sixth century would not have been so marked. The bishops of Rome, between Leo I. and Gregory the Great, were not in a position to concern themselves with the drift of ecclesiastical affairs in the islands of the north. But no sooner has Gregory accomplished his great revival and augmentation of the authority of the Roman see in western lands than the movement begins which gradually brings Ireland back within the confederation from which it had practically, though never formally or intentionally, been severed. The renewal of the union with continental Christianity in the seventh century was simply a return to the system established by Patrick and his coadjutors, and it would not be surprising if, in that period, men looked back with intenser interest to his work and exalted his memory more than ever.

It seems probable, as we saw, that the tendencies which asserted themselves after Patrick's death were partly of the nature of a relapse. Men went back to some practices which had been adopted in the Christian communities existent before his arrival on the scene. An old Easter reckoning, which he had attempted to supersede, was resumed. Perhaps, too, the Druidical tonsure from ear to ear had been used by earlier Irish Christians, and when it afterwards prevailed over the continental tonsure which he introduced, this was also a reversion to a pre-Patrician practice.

The work of Patrick may be illustrated by comparing him with other bearers of the same religion to peoples of northern and central Europe. He did not go among a folk entirely heathen, like Willibrord among the Frisians, or Adalbert among the western Slavs, or Bruno of Querfurt among the Patzinaks. The circumstances of his mission have some resemblance to those of Columba's mission in Caledonia. Columba went to organise and maintain Christianity among the Irish Dalriadan settlers and to convert the neighbouring Pictish heathen, just as Patrick went to organise as well as to propagate his faith. But while the conditions of their tasks had this similarity, their works are contrasted. It was the aim of Patrick to draw Ireland into close intimacy with continental Christianity, but Columba, who represented in Ireland tendencies opposed to the Patrician tradition, had no such aim, and he established a church in north Britain which offered a strenuous, though not long-protracted, resistance to unity.

The nearest likeness to Patrick will perhaps be found in St. Boniface, the Saxon Winfrith. He, too, like Patrick and Columba, had both to order and further his faith in regions where it was not unknown, and to introduce it into regions where it had never penetrated. But, like Patrick, and unlike Columba, he was in touch with the rest of western Christendom. The political and geographical circumstances were indeed different. Boniface was backed by the Frank monarchy; he was nearer Rome, in frequent communication with the Popes, and the Popes of that day had an authority far greater than the Popes before Gregory the Great. If Patrick looked with reverence to Rome as the apostolic seat, Boniface looked to Rome far more intently. In Patrick's day the Roman Empire meant a great deal more than the Roman see; in the days of Boniface the Pope was still a subject of the

Emperor, but the Emperor was far away in Constantinople, and to a bishop in Gaul or Britain it was the Bishop of Old Rome who, apart from the authority of his see, seemed to represent the traditions of Roman Christendom. But the work of Boniface and Patrick alike was to draw new lands within the pale of Christian unity, which was closely identified with the Roman name.

St Patrick did not do for the Scots what Wulfilas did for the Goths, and the Slavonic apostles for the Slavs; he did not translate the sacred books of his religion into Irish or found a national church literature. It is upon their literary achievements, more than on their successes in converting barbarians, that the fame of Wulfilas rests, and the fame of Cyril. The Gothic Bible of Wulfilas was available for the Vandals and other Germans whose speech was closely akin to Gothic. The importance of the Slavonic apostles, Cyril and his brother Methodius, is due to the fact that the literature which they initiated was available, not for the lands in which they laboured—Moravia and Pannonia, which no longer know them— but for Bulgaria and Russia. What Patrick, on the other hand, and his foreign fellow-workers did was to diffuse a knowledge of Latin in Ireland. To the circumstance that he adopted this line of policy, and did not attempt to create a national ecclesiastical language, must be ascribed the rise of the schools of learning which distinguished Ireland in the sixth and seventh centuries. From a national point of view the policy may be criticised; from a theologian's point of view the advantage may be urged of opening to the native clergy the whole body of patristic literature, and saving the trouble of translation and the chances of error. But the point is that the policy was entirely consonant with the development of western, as contrasted with eastern, Christianity. In the time of Patrick there was within the realm of the Emperor Theodosius II. a Syrian, as well as a Greek, ecclesiastical literature; in Armenia there was an Armenian; even in Egypt there was a Coptic; whereas in the realm of his cousin and colleague Valentinian III. there was only one ecclesiastical language, the speech of Rome itself. The reason was that Latin had become the universal language, not a mere *lingua franca,* in the western provinces, a fact which conditioned the whole growth of western Christendom. In the East, where this unity of tongue did not exist, no policy was adopted of imposing Greek on any new people which might be brought into ecclesiastical connexion with the Church of Constantinople. In the West the ideal of a common church language was formed, just because, within the Empire, there were no rivals to Latin, and so it was a matter of course, and not, at first, the result of a deliberate policy, that the Latin language and literature should accompany the Gospel. And this community of language powerfully conduced to the realisation of the *unitas ecclesiae.* The case of Ireland shows how potent this influence was. If Patrick had called into being for the Scots a sacred literature such as Cyril initiated for the Slavs, we may be sure that the tendencies in the Irish Church to strike out paths of development for itself, which were so strongly marked in the sixth century, would have been more effective and permanent in promoting isolation and aloofness, and that the successful movement of the following century which drew Ireland back into outward harmony and more active communion with the Western

Church would have been beset by far greater difficulties and might have been a failure. Even if the reform movement had been carried through in such conditions, there would have been the danger of a grave schism, like that which rent the Russian world in the seventeenth century when the reforms of Nicon the Patriarch were carried, but at the cost of dividing the Church for ever by the great *raskol*. The history of that episode illustrates the formidable resistance which a national sacred literature, partly consisting of, partly based on, translations, can offer to the ideal unity of a universal religion. If Greek had been originally established as the ecclesiastical language of Russia in the days of Vladimir, we may surmise that in the days of Alexius all national peculiarities and deviations which had been introduced in the meantime could have easily been corrected without causing the great split. On the other hand, if Gaelic had been established by Patrick as the ecclesiastical tongue of Ireland, the reformers who in the seventh century sought to abolish idiosyncrasies and restore uniformity might have caused a rupture in the Irish Church, which would have needed long years to heal. The Latin language is one of the *arcana imperii* of the Catholic Church.

It is true that the Irish Church moved on certain lines which Patrick did not contemplate and would not have approved. The development of the organisation which it was his task to institute was largely modified in colouring and conformation by the *genius terrae*. But it would be untrue to say that his work was undone. The schools of learning, for which the Scots became famous a few generations after his death, learning which contrasts with his own illiterateness,

owe their rise to the contact with Roman ideas and the acquaintance with Roman literature which his labours, more
than anything else, lifted within the horizon of Ireland. It
was not only the religion, but also the language which was
attached to it, that inaugurated a new period of culture for
the island, and opened a wider outlook on the universe. The
Irish were soon busily engaged in trying to work their own
past into the woof of ecumenical history, to synchronise their
insular memories with the annals of Rome and Greece, and
find a nook for their remote land in the story of the world.

These considerations may help to bring into relief the
place which Patrick holds in the history of Europe. Judged
by what he actually compassed, he must be placed along with
the most efficient of those who took part in spreading the
Christian faith beyond the boundaries of the Roman Empire. He was endowed in abundant measure with the quality
of enthusiasm, and stands in quite a different rank from the
apostle of England, in whom this victorious energy of enthusiasm was lacking, Augustine, the messenger and instrument
of Gregory the Great. Patrick was no mere messenger or
instrument. He had a strong personality and the power of
initiative; he depended on himself, or, as he would have said,
on divine guidance. He was not in constant communication
with Xystus, or Leo, or any superior; he was thrown upon the
resources of his own judgment. Yet no less than Augustine,
no less than Boniface, he was the bearer of the *Roman idea*.
But we must remember that it was the Roman idea of days
when the Church was still closely bound up in the Empire,
and owed her high prestige to the older institution which had
served as the model for her external organisation. The Pope

had not yet become a spiritual Caesar Augustus, as he is at
the present day. In the universal order, he was still for generations to be overshadowed by the Emperor. The Roman idea
at this stage meant not the idea of subjection to the Roman
see, but of Christianity as the religion of the Roman Empire.
It was as impossible for Patrick as it was impossible for the
High King of Ireland to divorce the idea of the Church from
the idea of the Empire. Christianity was marked off from all
other religions as the religion of the Romans in the wider
political sense of that Imperial name. If Christianity aspired
in theory to be ecumenical, Rome had aspired in theory
to realise universal sway before Christianity appeared. The
poet Claudian, in his brilliant sketch—written when Patrick
was a boy—of the amazing career of Rome, expresses her
ecumenical aspiration in the line—

Humanumque genus communi nomine fouit.[2]

That aspiration was destined to be fulfilled more completely
in another sense after her political decline. The dismemberment of the Empire and the upgrowth of the German
kingdoms brought about an evolution which enabled the
elder Rome to reassert her influence in a new way and a
new order. But it was the same idea, at different stages of
development, which was borne by Patrick, by Augustine, by
Boniface, and by Otto.

In this book an attempt has been made to complete the
picture of the transformation which was wrought in Europe, during the century succeeding the death of the great
Theodosius, by showing how, while the visible fabric of the
Empire was being undermined and disjointed, one corner

of Europe which its peace had never reached was brought within the invisible sway of its influence. We must remember that the phrase "dismemberment of the Empire" is far from embracing all the aspects of the momentous events which distinguish that eventful age. The process of Romanising was going foward actively at the same time. The German peoples who settled in the western provinces, at first as unwelcome subjects, soon to become independent nations, were submitted there to the influences of Roman culture, which were never more active and efficacious than when the political power of Rome was waning. As the Roman conquest of the Hellenic world had signified also that the Hellenic idea entered into a new phase of its influence, so the Teutonic occupation of western Europe meant a new sphere and a new mode of operation for the ideas which it was Rome's function and privilege to bestow upon mankind. And while Goths and Burgundians, and Franks and Suevians and Vandals, were passing on Roman soil, in greater or lesser degree, under the ascendency of an influence which was to be the making of some and perhaps the marring of others,—an influence which had begun before, but now became more intense,—the folks of Hiverne were reached by the same ineluctable force. But, while the Teutons came themselves into Rome's domain to claim and make good their rights in the imperial inheritance, the smaller share which was to fall to the Scots of Ireland was conveyed to their own gates. It was Patrick with his auxiliaries who bore to their shores the vessel of Rome's influence, along with the sacred mysteries of Rome's faith. No wonder that his labours should have been almost unobserved in the days of ecumenical stress and struggle, when the Germans by land and by sea were engaging the world's attention, and the Huns were rearing their vast though transient empire. But he was labouring for the Roman idea no less than the great Aetius himself, though in another way and on a smaller scene. He brought a new land into the spiritual federation which was so closely bound up with Rome, *nexuque pio longinqua reuinxit.*

NOTES

Preface

1 I may be permitted to remark that in vindicating the claims of history to be regarded as a science or *Wissenchaft,* I never meant to suggest a proposition so indefensible as that the presentation of the results of historical research is not an art, requiring the tact and skill in selection and arrangement which belong to the literary faculty. The friendly criticisms of Mr. John Morley in the *Nineteenth Century and After,* October 1904, and of Mr. S. H. Butcher in *Harvard Lectures on Greek Subjects* (1904), Lecture VI., show me that I did not sufficiently guard against this misapprehension.

Chapter I

1 For the expansion of Christianity in the first three centuries see Harnack's invaluable work *Die Mission und Ausbreitung des Christentums in den ersten drei Jahrhunderten* (1902).

2 Rufinus, *Hist. ecc.* ii. 7. For the Georgian legend of Nino see *Life of St. Nino,* translated by Marjory and J. O. Wardrop, in Oxford *Studia Biblica et Ecclesiastica,* vol. v. (1900).

3 *De Vocatione Gentium,* ii. 32.

4 On the other hand it may be questioned whether the army itself did anything to diffuse Christianity within the Empire. In the west certainly its chief significance in the history of religion was what it did to spread the solar, Mithraic worship. Cp. Harnack, *op. cit.* 268, 388.

5　Rufinus, *Hist. ecc.* i. 9.

6　Armenia was already Christian at the beginning of the fourth century in the days of Maximin.—Eusebius, *Hist. ecc.* ix. 8. 2.

7　Socrates, *Hist. ecc.* vii. 30

8　The island of Man is indeed another exception. The Scottic colonisation of north-western Britain (Argyle, etc.) was comparatively late, but before the middle of the fifth century (see below, chap. ix. p. 192).

9　Professor Rhŷs thinks that it was to Ireland, more than to Britain, that the Gallic Druids went to learn their art, and that Caesar (in *B.G.* vi. 13) was badly informed; and he has recently stated this view in *Studies in Early Irish History* (*Proceedings of British Academy*, vol. i.), p. 35. It is remarkable that, apart from Caesar's assertion, the only evidence for Druidism in southern Britain pertains to the island of Anglesey (Tacitus, *Ann.* xiv. 29), and Professor Rhŷs holds that in the first century A.D. Anglesey (Mona) was not yet Brythonic. Druidism in the Isle of Man is attested by a stone inscribed *Dovaidona maqi Droata* "(the burial-place) of Dovaido, son of (the) Druid." See Professor Rhŷs in the *Academy* for August 15, 1890.

10　Tacitus, *Agricola,* c. 24, medio inter Britanniam atque Hispaniam sita. Cp. Caesar, *B.G.* v. 13. The notice in Orosius (*Hist.* i. 2, § 72) of the lighthouse at Brigantia in north-western Spain as built *ad speculam Britanniae* is noteworthy. Compare the remarks of Professor Rhŷs, *op. cit.* p. 47.

11　Tacitus, *ib.* aditus portusque per commercia et negotiatores cogniti.

12　Tacitus, *ib.* The policy recommended by Agricola, who considered one legion sufficient to hold the island, was based partly on the ground of political expedience. The conquest of Ireland, he thought, would have a similar wholesome effect on Britain to that which the conquest of Britain had on Gaul, by removing the spectacle of liberty (*si Romana ubique arma et uelut e conspectu libertas tolleretur*).

13　The baronies of Upper and Lower Deece, in Co. Meath.

14 Decies within Drum, and Decies without Drum, in Co. Waterford.

15 It seems probable that Pelagius sprang from these Gaelic settlers in Britain. See p. 35.

16 See below, cap. viii. *ad fin.*

17 Un peuple n'emprunte pas l'alphabet des voisins s'il n'a pas à correspondre avec eux. ... Qui donc constate un emprunt de monnaie et d'alphabet, en tous temps et en tous lieux, peut affirmer un échange de produits et d'idées (V. Bérard, *Les Phéniciens et l'Odyssée,* i. p. 20).

Chapter II

1 There is no evidence, and no probability, that the name Paul was adopted on his conversion, or that it had anything to do with Sergius Paullus.

2 Frigeridus is Gothic Frigairêths.

3 Croagh Patrick, close to Westport.

4 Dalriada = north Antrim; Dalaradia = south Antrim and Down. The Latin form, Ulidia, is used in this book for Ulaid in the narrower meaning.

5 It has been conjectured that Miliucc's dwelling was on the hill of Skerry, on the northern side of the Braid; see p. 70.

6 The association of Saint Elias with the sun was due to the resemblance of the name to the Greek ἥλιος

Chapter III

1 St. Honorat.—Lero is Ste. Marguerite.

2 A.D. 426.

3 A.D. 433.

4 His own expression "as a son" shows that *parentes* here means kinsfolk, not parents, and justifies the inference that his parents were dead.

5 Pelagius, *Letter to Demetrias,* Migne, *P.L.*, xxxii. 1100.

6   Prosper has an epigram on the thesis that the whole life of non-Christians is sin:

> Perque omnes calles errat sapientia mundi.
> Et tenebris addit quae sine luce gerit.
>
> (*Epig.* 83, ed. Migne, 51, p. 524.)

7   Compare Celestine, *Ep.* iv. (Migne, *P.L.*, l. 434), nullus inuitis detur episcopus.

8   The conjecture is due to Professor Zimmer.

9   The old kingdom of Leinster, or Laigin, was south of the Liffey, and in this book "Leinster" is used in this sense (not equivalent to the modern province, which includes the old kingdom of Meath). See below, chap. iv.

10 No better illustration of this can be found than Pope Gregory's provision, for the mission of Augustine to England, as recorded in Bede, *Hist. ecc.* i. 29; he sent, besides fellow-workers, "uniuersa quae ad cultum erant ac ministerium ecclesiae necessaria, uasa videlicet sacra, et vestimenta altarium, ornamenta quoque ecclesiarum, et sacerdotalia uel clericilia indumenta, sanctorum etiam apostolorum ac martyrum reliquias, necnon et codices plurimos."

11 It has recently been held, more plausibly but erroneously, that Patrick was on his way to Rome when the news of the death of Palladius overtook him.

12 Celestine probably died July 27, and Xystus succeeded July 31, 432. These dates have been determined by M. Duchesne, *Liber Pontificalis,* i. pp. ccli.-ii.

13 It is probable that excommunication by a Roman bishop was also recognised as universally binding. The question whether the popes had the right of annulling sentences pronounced by provincial councils on bishops, depends on the question of the authenticity of the Council of Sardica. See J. Friedrich, *Sitzungsber.* of the Bavarian Academy, 1901, 417 *sqq.*; E. Babut, *Le concile de Turin,* 75.

14 A.D. 366–384.

15 See Babut, *Le concile de Turin* (1904), a valuable work.

16 This has been well brought out by M. Babut.

17 *Novella,* xvi.
18 *Commonitorium,* ii. 33, 34.

Chapter IV

1 The chief source for the social and economic conditions of ancient Ireland is the collection of the *Ancient Laws of Ireland* (6 vols., 1865–1901). A clear account of the general framework of society, with interesting details and illustrations, will be found in Dr. Joyce's *Social History of Ireland,* vol. i.
2 *Tuath* = people, tribe, tribal district.
3 *Flaith* = noble.
4 The *bó-aires.*
5 The tributes and presents which are due from the under-kings to the over-kings, the donations which the over-kings owe to the under-kings, the privileges which the various kings possess, are the subject of the *Book of Rights* (edited and translated by O'Donovan, 1847), which still awaits a critical investigation. It is easy to see that it was compiled in Munster in the tenth century, but it was based on older material of high antiquity, and clearly reproduces the general character of the mutual relations which theoretically bound together the Irish kingdoms.
6 The king of Aileach was so called because his palace was at Aileach, near Londonderry. His territory was north Ulster to the Bann. Ulaid was east Ulster; Oriel, south Ulster.
7 This is clearly to be inferred from the *Book of Rights,* where no relations or mutual obligations are mentioned as existing between the three Ulster kings. Nor was there, since the destruction of the old Ulidian kingdom in the third century, any name to designate the whole province, for Ulaid was confined to the kingdom in the east of Ulster. The use of Ultonia to describe the province, as distinguished from Ulidia = Ulaid, is of course merely a literary convention.
8 See Petrie, *Tara Hill,* 135.
9 His date, according to the Annals, was A.D. 358–366; Niall reigned A.D. 379–405; his nephew, Dathi, 405–428; and then his son,

Loigaire, 428–463. For Amolngaid (Dathi's brother), king of Connaught.

10 Tyr-connell.

11 The derivation of the word *druid* (nom. *drui,* gen. *druad*) is uncertain. Perhaps, as Professor Rhŷs holds, Druidism was not of Celtic origin, and the word "was adopted by the Celts from some earlier population conquered by them" (see his "Studies in Early Irish History," in *Proceedings of the British Academy,* vol. i. p. 8). *Druidecht* is the Irish for magic. For the functions and powers of the Druids some excellent pages in Dr. Joyce's *Social History,* I. c. ix., may be recommended; illustrations and references will be found there.

12 Mug Ruith, servant of the wheel, was the name of a mythical Druid.

13 The *Feth Fiada.*

14 For these superstitious ceremonies at baptism cp. Duchesne, *Origines du culte chrétien,* pp. 296–7 (the exorcism of salt), 299, 317; cp. 349.

15 In the remarkable ancient Irish Christian incantation, the Lorica, ascribed to St Patrick, the Trinity, Angels, Prophets, and other Christian powers are invoked, but also "might of heaven, brightness of sun, brilliance of moon, splendour of fire, speed of light, swiftness of wind, depth of sea, stability of earth, firmness of rock," to intervene between him who repeats the spell when he arises in the morning and "every fierce merciless force that may come upon my body and soul; against incantations of false prophets, against black laws of paganism, against false laws of heresy, against deceit of idolatry, *against spells of women and smiths and druids,* against all knowledge that is forbidden [so Atkinson] the human soul."

16 M. Réville, dealing with the third century, puts this very well. "Chacun croit sans le moindre difficulté à toutes les merveilles et à toutes les folies. On dirait même que plus une pratique est merveilleuse, plus elle a de chance d'être admise sans contestation. Chose singulière! les adeptes des religions opposées ne contestent pas la réalité des miracles allégués par leurs adversaires: Celse

admet les miracles des chrétiens, et ceux-ci ne se refusent pas
à admettre les miracles païens; des deux parts on attribue aux
mauvais esprits les merveilles invoquées par les adversaires" (*La
Religion à Rome sous les Sévères*, p. 131).

Chapter V

1 The *Memoir* by Tírechán.
2 The *Life* by Muirchu.
3 Cuchullin of legend.
4 Then called Brene Strait.
5 The Slaney. It flows from L. Money past Raholp.
6 It has been conjectured that the stronghold of Miliucc was on the
   hill of Skerry, north of Slemish, on the other side of the Braid
   valley. Muirchu says that Patrick saw the conflagration from the
   south side of Slemish. We may interpret south to mean south-west.
   A cross, mentioned by Muirchu, was erected on the spot where
   the legend supposed Patrick to have stood, and the memory of
   this is still preserved in the name of the townland of Cross, on a
   hill to the west of Slemish.
7 Dr. W. Stokes, taking the story literally, suggests that Miliucc
   committed self-destruction as "a mode of vengeance" (*Book of
   Lismore*, p. 295).
8 *Mag-inis,* later known as Lecale (*Leath Cathuil*), now the baronies
   of Lower and Upper Lecale. It is accurately described as a penin-
   sular plain.
9 But meaning *barn.*
10 There is a second story (also recorded by Muirchu), clearly inspired
   by the same motive. Patrick was resting near Druimbo (in the
   north of Mag Inis, and close to a salt marsh), and he heard the
   noise of pagans who were busily engaged in making an earthwork.
   It was Sunday and he commanded them to cease from work.
   When they refused he cursed them: "Mudebrod! may your work
   not profit you!" and the sea rushed in, as in the other story, and
   the work was destroyed. The curse *mudebrod* (or *mudebroth*) has
   not been explained.

Chapter VI

1   See above, chap. i. p. 14.

2   See above, chap. iv. p. 72.

3   Compare what has been said above in chap. i. p. 9.

4   This name is the same as the British Vortigern (Welsh Gwrtheyrn), and the original Goidelic form was similar. It occurs in Ogam inscriptions, thus: ... Maqi Vorrtigern<i>, on a stone of Ballyhank (near Cork), now in the Dublin Museum (Rhŷs, *Proc. of R.S.A.I.,* pt. i. vol. xxxii. p. 9, 1902).

5   The distance of Tara from Slane is about ten miles.

6   Yet more remote from the Paschal season was the feast of Samhain at the close of autumn (November 1), when on the hill of Tlachtga, not far from Trim, a fire was kindled, from which, tradition says, all hearths in Ireland were lit. It was at Samhain too, according to tradition, that the High Kings used to hold such high festivals at Tara as are designated in the story.

7   This incident is obviously suggested by St. John xx. 19, 26. When St. Columba went to the palace of King Brude the closed gates opened of their own accord (Adamnan, *V. Col,* ii. 35).

8   Tírechán, p. 308, perrexitque ad civitatem Temro ad Loigairium filium Neill iterum quia apud illum foedus pepigit ut non occideretur in regno illius.

9   At Crag, in Co. Kerry.—Macalister, *Studies in Irish Epigraphy,* ii. p. 52.

10 It should be Donagh-shaughlin, for Donagh is *domnach,* a church, whereas *dún* is a fort. There is no doubt that Dun here is a corruption, as we get the form Donnaclsacheling in a document of A.D. 1216 (Reeves, *Eccl. Ant.* p. 128).

11 The *Confession* shows that this comparison was sometimes in Patrick's mind.

12 Perfectam vitam, *Hymn* v. 4. Secundinus died A.D. 447, acc. to *Ann. Ult.*

13 Telltown comes by popular etymology from the genitive Taillteann. The site is marked by a round rath. O'Donovan said in

1856 that it had been in recent times a resort for the men of Meath for hurling, wrestling, and other sports (*Four Masters,* i. p. 22).

14 Herbord, *Vit. Ott.* ii. 14. The silence of early authorities is decisive against the isolated statement that Patrick preached at Taillte against the "burning of the firstborn offspring."

15 Mac Fechach.—Tírechán, 310_{24}.

16 Áth Brón.—Tír. 307_{28}.

17 St. Colomb's House. For its description and measurements see Petrie (*Round Towers,* 430–31), who compares it with St. Kevin's House at Glendalough, and Dunraven's *Notes on Irish Architecture,* vol. ii. p. 50 (plans and photograph).

18 Tírechán, 310–11.

19 It may be observed that if the idol of Mag Slecht had been eminently important for all Ireland, and had been destroyed at a period subsequent to St Patrick, there could hardly fail to be a Christian record of its fall. In the *Annals of the Four Masters,* s.a. 464, it is said that Conall, son of Niall, ancestor of the lords of Tyrconnell, was done to death by the "old Folks" of Mag Slecht, who caught him unprotected. The thought occurs that Conall had supported the attack on the worship of Cenn Cruaich, and that his death was an act of vengeance wreaked by people of the plain who still clung to the old faith.

Chapter VII

1 Perhaps A.D. 444–5.

2 At Duma Graid, close to Lake Kilglass. See Tírechán, 313, and *Vit. Trip.* p. 94.

3 Between Sligo and Leitrim.

4 May the name be the same as that of the tribe of the Anghaile (Annaly), who extended their power subsequently into Tethbia (cp. O'Donovan, *Book of Rights,* p. 11, *note*)?

5 Tamnach.

6 "Church of Bishop Brón."

7 Ciarrigi. Through the baronies of Costello, Clanmorris, and Kil-maine. Possibly Aghamore, south of Kilkelly, may lie on the supposed route. It has been conjectured that the church *in campo Nairniu* (Tírechán, 321) was there.

8 In quo fiunt episcopi.

9 Muiriscc (*Muir* = sea) Aigli. (The promontory dominated by Knocknaree in Sligo Bay was also called Muiriscc, Tír. 327.) The promontory was also known as Umail. This name is preserved in the *Owles,* designating the regions on both sides of Clew Bay, now the baronies of Murrisk and Burris-*hoole*; the latter word also contains the name Umail.

10 Its height is 2510 feet. Mount Nephin, close to Lake Conn, is higher.

11 Carrick-on-Shannon.

12 He first went to a place called Duma Graid, and ordained there the arch-presbyter Ailbe, who resided at Shancoe (as mentioned above). It may be suspected that the name Duma Graid (for which we expect a modern Doogary) is preserved in Dockery's Island, near the mouth of Lake Kilglass.

13 Tuatha De Danann, people of the goddess Danann. They are said, in the mythical history of Ireland, to have colonised the country and to have been conquered by the Milesians.

14 Fountain of Clebach.

15 Selce has not been identified.

16 Kill-araght. From here Patrick may have revisited Mag Airthic and the Kerries.

17 *Irrus* Domnand, "the peninsula of Domnu" = barony of *Erris* in Mayo. Cp. Rhŷs, "Studies in Early Irish History," p. 38.

18 Ballina.

19 It was one of the many Donaghmores, "great churches," which Patrick is said to have founded. He consigned it to the care of Mucneus.

20 The name of a townland, in which there is an old churchyard and traces of ruins, to the right of the road from Ballina to Killala, a mile south of Killala. For Donaghmore and Mullaghfarry

(*farry* = *forrach* = *foirrgea*, Tír. 327) see O'Donovan, *Hy Fiachrach,*
pp. 466 and 467, notes.

Chapter VIII

1 *De laude sanctorum* (Migne, *Patr. Lat.* xx.).
2 Jerome, *Adversus Vigilantium,* c. 5.
3 A.D. 440.
4 See above, chap. iii. p. 64.
5 It may be Ptolemy's *Regia* ('Ρηγία). Cp. Rhŷs, "Studies in Early
   Irish History," p. 49 (*Proc. of British Acad.* vol. i.).
6 The dimensions of these houses are given, *Vit. Trip.* p. 226:—
   "27 feet in the Great House, 17 feet in the kitchen, 7 feet in the
   oratory [*aregal,* supposed to be derived from *oraculum*]; and it was
   thus that he used always to found the *congbala*" [*i.e.* the sacred
   enclosures, or cloisters]. If these houses were circular, the numbers
   represent the diameters. For the topography of Armagh see the
   paper of Reeves, *The Ancient Churches of Armagh* (Lusk, 1860),
   with a plan. The locality of the first settlement, *ubi nunc est Fertae
   martyrum,* "the grave of the relics" (Muirchu, 290), he fixes, by
   means of the monastery of Temple-fertagh, which existed at the
   beginning of the seventeenth century, to the land south of Scotch
   St., near Scotch St. river (p. 10).
7 The two stages, first below, and then on the hill, are doubtless
   historical. We may conjecture that the second and final foundation
   is that which is recorded in the Annals, and that the first settlement
   had been made before the visit to Rome.
8 This is expressed by *quantum habeo,* "so far as it is mine," in
   Muirchu, [2]292$_{31}$.
9 There can be little question that the (contemporary) expression
   in provincia nostra in *Ann. Ult.,* A.D. 443, means "in Ireland,"
   conceived as a single ecclesiastical province, like the province of a
   metropolitan.
10 Láthrach Patricc (*Trip.* 349$_8$). Cp. Reeves, *Antiquities of Down and
   Connor,* pp. 47 and 236; for Glore, *ib.* 87, 338; for Dunseveric, *ib.*
   286. For Clogher and Ard-Patrick (Louth).

11 *Ep. against Corot.* 375.

12 *Ánn, Ult.,* A.D. 439.

13 Or Killishea.

14 Áth Fithot, south of Tallow.

15 Old Kilcullen, south of (new) Kilcullen, in Co. Kildare.

16 In barony of Slievemargy, in Queen's County, a mile or so north-west of the town of Carlow.

17 Generally described inaccurately as the Acts of a Synod.

18 For this sphere of Christian activity in the early Church see Harnack, *Mission und Ausbreitung des Christentums,* p. 120.

19 A Christian who believes in a supernatural female form (*lamia quae interpretatur striga*) seen in a mirror is to be anathematised. One is reminded of

>   Was seh' ich? Welch ein himmlisch Bild
>   Zeigt sich in diesem Zauberspiegel! (Goethe, *Faust,* Part I.)

20 Chap. iii. pp. 61 *sqq.*

21 Collection of Irish Canons, 20. 5. b (ed.^{2} Wasserschleben, p. 61). For the possible date of the canon, and for some further illustration of the subject.

22 *Confession,* 368$_9$.

23 *Ib.* 372$_{17}$; cp. 367$_{13}$.

24 *Ib.* 368$_{26}$.

25 Otto of Bamberg is said to have baptized 22,156 converts in Pomerania during his first journey! Mon. Prieflingensis, *V. Ott.* ii. 20; Ebbo, *V. Ott.* ii. 11.

26 *Confession,* 369$_{22}$.

27 *Confession,* 367$_{16}$.

28 *Ib* 372. It may be conjectured, from the context, that this happened in Connaught.

29 So Otto of Bamberg used to distribute presents in Pomerania as a means of propagating Christianity, Herbord, *Dial.* 2. 7.

30 The question arises, Where did Patrick get his money? Did he inherit from his father? It is useless to ask.

31 *Confession,* 371$_{25}$.

32 See the anecdote in Tírechán, p. 303.

33 Epistles of Gregory, vi. 10 (A.D. 595), *M.G.H.* vol. i. p. 389.

34 Todd, *St Patrick,* p. 154.

35 The early abbots of Hi (Iona) were almost entirely chosen from a branch of the family of Tirconnell (Reeves, *Adamnan,* genealogical table, p. 342).

36 See the bequest of Fith Fio in *Lib. Arm.* (*Trip.* 338). It is added that if there be no suitable person in the community of Drumlease, some one from Patrick's community (Armagh, or any Patrician community?) should be chosen.

37 *Corus Bescna,* p. 73 (*Ancient Laws of Ireland,* vol. iii.).

38 Tírechán, 330_{29}, *fecit alteram* (*aeclessiam*) *hi Tortena orientali in qua gens oThig Cirpani, sed libere semper.* Cp. 321_7.

39 *Additional Notices* in *Lib. Arm.* (338_4, *liberauit rex Deo et Patricio*). The exact boundaries of the land are given, as if from the original document. Two interests were concerned here, that of Caichán and that of MacCairthin, and the land is described as "Caichán's Fifth." The two men are designated as *flaith* (lord) and *aithech* (tenant-farmer?), and they jointly devoted the land to ecclesiastical use.

40 *Corus Bescna,* p. 73.

41 *Ib.* p. 71.

42 Cp. *Ancient Laws,* iii., Introd. p. lxxii.

43 *Ib.* luii., *Corus B.* pp. 41, 43.

44 *Ib.* pp. 39–43.

45 Cp. Introd. pp. luiii. *sqq.*

46 Todd, *St Patrick,* 51 *sqq.*

47 See above, chap. vii. p. 143.

48 It has twenty-one letters, a b c d e f g h i l m n o p q r s t u v, and ng (a guttural nasal, which occurs in the name *Amolngaid*; cp. the Greek double gamma). If the Goidels had originally invented an alphabet to suit their own language they would never have constructed this. They had to resort to various devices to represent their sounds by its means.

49 More strictly, a new letter was added, and *u* was differentiated into two, to represent its two sounds. It is as well to say that in describing the ogams as a cipher it is not intended to imply that they were cryptic, but only that they were not an independent alphabet.

50 For the Iberian alphabet see Hübner's *Monumenta linguae Ibericae* (1893). Cp. Strabo, 3. 1. 6.

51 *B.G.* vi. 14.

52 Desjardins, *Géographie de la Gaule,* ii. 214, note 3.

Chapter IX

1 Ail Clúade.

2 *Milites.*

3 *Conf.* 360$_8$.

4 Cp. *Letter, ad init., inter barbaras itaque gentes habito proselitus et profuga.*

5 *Conf.* 374$_{29}$. Compare 357$_{15}$.

6 *Conf.* 370$_2$. The passage 373$_{5-9}$ also supports the view in the text. In that passage the oldest MS. has *ab aliquo uestro*; and we should probably read *uestrum* with the later MSS.

7 *Ib.* 359$_2$.

8 *Ib.* 372$_{31}$.

9 See above, chap. iii. p. 53.

10 This is the theory of Professor Zimmer.

11 The Second Letter to the Corinthians seems to have been especially before him. This was natural. In it Paul was vindicating his character.

12 The legend will be found in *Vit. Trip.* pp. 112 *sqq.*

13 The old lists of the Armagh succession agree in assigning to Benignus ten years as bishop, so that, as Benignus died in 467 (*Ann. Ult., sub anno*), he would have succeeded in 457.

14 March 17.

15 Oirthir, not to be confounded with the kingdom of Oriel (Oirgéill), of which it formed the eastern portion.

16 Inundations are a recurring motive in the legends of the Island-plain. See the salt-marsh stories, see p. 74.

17 This second incident can be shown to be a subsequent invention.

18 This story is also told by Muirchu, but not in immediate connexion with the story of the waggon and oxen seized by the men of Orior. It seems probable that the latter was suggested by the

former. We meet the duplicate waggon and oxen in the Life of St. Abban (Colgan, *Acta Sanctorum,* i. March 16, cc. 41 *sqq.*), where the account of that saint's death and burial and the struggle between the north and the south Leinster men is obviously borrowed from the stories about St Patrick. Another story of wild bulls drawing a saint's body to its tomb will be found in the Life of St. Melorus of Cornwall, *Acta Sanctorum* (Boll.), Jan. 1, vol. i. p. 136.

19 It is to be seen in the National Museum at Dublin. For the evidence as to the bell and the staff. For the copy of the gospels, which used falsely to be supposed to be his.

Chapter X

1 Except in regard to Britain, and the British Church was similarly isolated.

2 *De Cons. Stil. Lib.* iii. l. 151.